eat * sleep * shop

COPENHAGEN
STYLE GUIDE

ANNA PEUCKERT & SØREN JEPSEN

MURDOCH BOOKS
SYDNEY · LONDON

N

COPENHAGEN

CONTENTS

WELCOME!

The Danes are the happiest people in the world! This has been confirmed again and again by a great many studies, and we are only too happy to believe them. After all, anybody who has ever strolled through the Danish capital on a sunny day will understand why: there's plenty of exciting architecture, sparkling waterways and friendly, good-looking people on bicycles everywhere.

Copenhagen is a young city, and big enough to attract people from all over the world, yet compact enough to be comfortably explored on foot or by bicycle. This city on the Øresund represents a lot of what makes little Denmark such an appealing place, including not only world-famous design and great fashion, but also a virtually unequalled level of sustainability.

If you spend a little time in the city, it's easy to find many examples of uniquely Danish serenity. There are lots of children out and about, being carted through the city on cargo bicycles by their hip urban parents. Prams parked outside shops and cafés are a common sight, with cosily rugged up little bundles inside, happily sleeping. The Danes agree that fresh air is great for babies and leave them to snooze outside under warm blankets, while their parents enjoy their caffè lattes inside.

Danish fashion, which is rightly renowned all over the world, is another expression of this calm attitude. It exudes high quality, shows careful, loving attention to detail, and is never, ever loud or ostentatious. Most Danish fashion features muted colours, and there is black everywhere. But the way the Danes do it, it never gets boring—they are too dedicated to outstanding quality and smart design. To put it succinctly: Copenhagen dresses elegantly and timelessly.

Even when the weather starts getting a bit cold and dreary in autumn, the clever Danes have the perfect antidote, for which they even invented an endearing, virtually untranslatable word: *hygge*. *Hygge* means, more or less, 'the total absence of anything annoying or disruptive' and describes comfy, candlelit homes, with good company and good food. It sounds great and is guaranteed to bring happiness, so it's time for us to find out why all of this is so easily accessible in the Danish capital.

Copenhagen Style Guide is your indispensable guide for exploring this lovable city on the sea. In this little book, we take you to the most exciting shops, best restaurants and hippest art galleries, steering well clear of the well-trodden tourist paths. Join us in exploring the busy *Torvehallerne* market halls (p. 86), a unique shop selling typefaces (*Playtype Concept Store*, p. 235), cosy cafés (*Den Plettede Gris,* p. 110) and a hotel straight out of another time (*Hotel Alexandra*, p. 82), among plenty more.

Velkommen til København!

COPENHAGEN CITY TIPS

Bicycles

Copenhagen might just be the world's most bicycle-crazy city—together with Amsterdam—and so there's no better way to explore the Danish capital than on two wheels. Bicycle paths are often wider than footpaths, and there are veritable bicycle freeways along major routes, including the Cykelslangen ('bicycle snake'), which takes cyclists across the harbour. If you don't feel very confident, just stick to the quieter side streets. Most hotels offer bicycles for hire, and *www.bycyklen.dk* has bike hire depots all over the city.

Public transport

Copenhagen's small metro network is currently being extended in a major way, and for the time being you may need to use buses instead of trains for some of our suggested tours until the new lines have been completed. Buses operate frequently; they are on time and can be used with the same tickets as regional and metro trains. It's best to buy single tickets, or get a Rejsekort Anonymt at one of the ticket machines if you're planning to use buses and trains a bit. These plastic cards come at a one-off price of €10 as credit for your trips. Be sure to carry a valid ticket: inspectors in Copenhagen are merciless!

Food

Copenhagen deservedly enjoys an excellent international reputation for its culinary culture. At the time of print, fifteen restaurants carry at least one Michelin star, and noma, the world's best restaurant according to the highly respected San Pellegrino List, also calls Copenhagen home. Yet dining out in Copenhagen does not need to be expensive: there are plenty of small, inexpensive restaurants that pride themselves on cooking with fresh, high-quality, often organic produce. Smørrebrød is a classic Danish dish that has been enjoying a major revival, and hot dogs, the Danish fast food classic, can be bought cheaply all over the city.

Prices

Copenhagen has never really moved far from the top in international rankings of the world's most expensive cities. Converting Danish krone into euros, pounds or dollars can be tedious. It might be useful to download a currency conversion app to your mobile phone to make things easier. However, cash is rapidly losing relevance in Denmark—you can pay even very small amounts with a credit or Maestro card, from a takeaway coffee to a taxi ride.

Tipping

This, at least, is one area where Denmark is less costly than many other countries—tipping is highly unusual. Local waiting and service staff are well paid and generally do not expect customers to round up payment. The same applies to taxi drivers, spa and hotel staff. Of course they will be happy to accept a little extra if you're really thrilled about the service you received, but tips should not exceed ten per cent of the total cost.

Boats

There's water everywhere in Copenhagen, as the city lies close to the sea and features a number of lakes. It therefore comes as no surprise that a boat cruise is one of the best ways to explore the city. A great way to do this is to take one of the water taxis connecting the Royal Danish Library—known as the

'Black Diamond'—with the Little Mermaid. You can travel on these taxis with a standard bus ticket. If you prefer a proper city cruise, take one of the Netto boats, which are also quite inexpensive and have good tour guides on board. Tours are available in a number of languages.

Weather

As in the other Scandinavian countries, winters in Copenhagen tend to be quite gloomy and long; the sky generally stays grey during the colder months, and days are very short. All the more reason for the Danes to venture out to their parks and beaches any time there's even a glimpse of sunshine. July and August are the sunniest months, but many restaurants keep their outdoor seating areas open until late autumn, despite cool temperatures.

LGBT

Denmark was the world's first country to recognise same-sex partnerships legally, in 1989. Gay and lesbian couples have been able to adopt children since 2009, and full marriage equality between heterosexual and homosexual couples was legislated in 2012. This means that gay and lesbian couples are able to get married in church, which has been a major boost to LGBT wedding tourism. Copenhagen is the centre of the Danish LGBT movement; the city has hosted the Gay Games and celebrates Copenhagen Pride every August.

Nightlife

Copenhagen is a relaxed city full of people who love going out. But there's no need to dress to the hilt when going out, as most clubs have a very relaxed door policy. After all, the city's best parties are found on its streets and squares.

Street parties tend to dominate Copenhagen's calendar of events particularly during the summer months, culminating in the four-day Distortion festival in June, which takes place on the streets of a different suburb every day. For information about upcoming events visit *www.aok.dk/english.*

Opening hours

While some regulations regarding shopping hours are more relaxed in Denmark than in other European countries (shops may open on Sundays and public holidays, for example) standard business hours are relatively short. Most shops open around 10 am and close again around 6 pm; on weekends they usually stay open only until 4 pm. Copenhagen's late shopping day is traditionally Friday, with many shops doing business until at least 7 or 8 pm. There are no curfews or opening hour restrictions for the city's bars and clubs.

Souvenirs

Smørrebrød is not a great thing to take back home in your hand luggage, so let us suggest a few alternative ideas for lovely souvenirs from Copenhagen: invest in a piece of design history and buy one of Kay Bojesen's wooden animal figures, which you'll treasure for life. Or treat yourself to a piece of Danish fashion by Stine Goya, Henrik Vibskov or Wood Wood, which can be difficult to find outside the country. If you fancy a culinary souvenir, you just can't go past good Danish liquorice, and Johan Bülow makes the city's best.

12-HOUR BUCKET LIST

Our website, *12hrs.net*, takes readers on quick tours of the world's most exciting cities—one travel guide for twelve hours per city. Our approach to the website is similar to this book: both focus on design, fashion and attractions off the beaten tourist tracks.

Our perfect day in Copenhagen would start with a delicious bowl of porridge in *Grød* (p. 130) in Nørrebro district. As we'll have a busy day ahead, a nourishing breakfast is a must. We'll then head to *Superkilen* (p. 148), a colourful park and architectural playground in the district's northwest. We're bound to take plenty of Instagram pics of the red section of the installation. Let's then stroll through the picturesque *Assistens Kirkegård* cemetery (p. 141), a veritable urban oasis, to get back to the centre of Nørrebro.

This is where we turn our minds to shopping. Our first stop is *Adelié* (p. 154), a store run by fashion blogger Tikkie Oestrich Iversen, who has an infallible flair for new trends and sells fashion by mainly Danish designers. We'll then go bargain hunting at the *Acne Archive* (p. 146) and the *Wood Wood Museum* (p. 85), two outlet stores that are anything but trashy.

A quick coffee in the *Kaffebar* (p. 147) on Elmegade should boost energy levels in preparation for a stroll through the *Torvehallerne* market halls (p. 86) before

it's time to have lunch in the *Atelier September* (p. 22). We recommend the avocado on rye with lemon and chilli while watching passers-by. After that, we suggest a leisurely browse through *Henrik Vibskov* (p. 56), *Wood Wood* (p. 36) and *Storm* (p. 44). Visit *HAN Kjøbenhavn* (p. 48) to try out some sophisticated scents by Le Labo before moving on to Scandinavian fashion designs from *Stine Goya* (p. 18), *Acne* (p. 67) and *Norse Projects* (p. 68).

But we don't want to spend all day shopping, so let's take a little detour walking from the shopping strip to the waterfront. This takes us past the *Royal Palace*, where we may be lucky enough to see the changing of the Royal Guard, and on to the *Opera* and *National Theatre*—simply exquisite Danish architecture! We stroll on through the picturesque district of *Nyhavn* towards the hotel *SP34* (p. 90), the perfect place for putting our shopping bags down and our feet up before getting changed for the evening.

We suggest an utterly delectable dinner at *Höst* (p. 88)—bookings recommended. After dinner and some wonderful wine, it'll be time to move on to the meat-packing district for drinks and dance music at *Bakken* (p. 216) to round off a splendid day.

And this is how twelve amazing hours in Copenhagen can just fly by.

KØBENHAVN K

N

Copenhagen's inner city, which locals usually refer to simply as København K, is the city's living heart. This is where you'll find not only the major museums, art galleries and tourist attractions, but also where you should set out from if you're after a Copenhagen shopping spree. Between the Tivoli and the old Kastellet citadel you'll find an incredibly diverse range of shops, from high-fashion boutiques to charming second-hand bazaars, from designer furniture stores to holes in the wall selling tasty homemade food specialties.

SHOPS

1 Keramik og Glasværkstedet
2 Stine Goya
3 Le Beau Marché
5 Tage Andersen
8 Magasin
9 Birger Christensen
11 Jane Kønig
14 Wood Wood
16 NN07
17 Casa Shop
18 Rue Verte
19 Ganni
20 Storm
21 Ørgreen Optics
22 Bering House of Flowers
23 HAN Kjøbenhavn
24 Baum und Pferdgarten
26 Time's Up Vintage
27 Henrik Vibskov
29 Wardrobe 19
30 Project 4
31 Summerbird
32 Perch's
34 Acne
35 Norse Projects
36 Maria Black
37 Illums Bolighus
38 Illum
40 HAY House
43 Pede & Stoffer Mens
46 Wasteland
48 København K
49 Wood Wood Museum

ARTS & CULTURE

10 Kunsthal Charlottenborg
13 Designmuseum Danmark
53 Ny Carlsberg Glyptotek

CAFÉS

4 Atelier September
15 Kaf Bar
28 Democratic Coffee Bar
39 The Royal Café
44 La Glace

FOOD

7 Llama
12 The Standard
25 DØP—The Organic
    Hot Dog Stand
41 Condesa
45 Greasy Spoon
50 Torvehallerne
51 Höst
54 Toldboden

NIGHTLIFE

33 The Jane
42 Ruby

HOTELS

6 Generator Hostel
47 Hotel Alexandra
52 SP34

1 Keramik og Glasværkstedet

This small shop directly next to the city centre is Scandinavian through and through. The tall front windows let in plenty of light, and all of the pieces are lovingly displayed on wide windowsills, tables and shelves. Keramik og Glasværkstedet is where four Danish glass and ceramics artists—among them Annemette Kissow, who designs the porcelain collection for the Danish design company Vipp—sell their treasures.

Kronprinsessegade 43, 1306 København K
www.keramikogglasvaerkstedet.dk

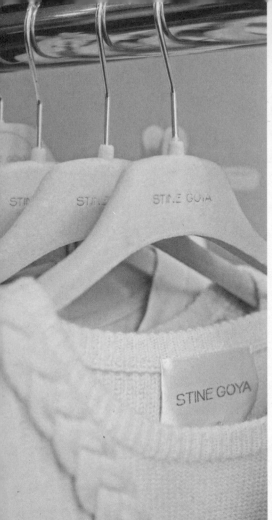

2 Stine Goya

Stine Goya, the adorable darling of the
Danish fashion industry, sells parts of
her current collection and some selected
accessories in her tiny flagship store in
Gothersgade. Goya, a former model,
is known for designing fashion that she
would love to wear herself, featuring
pastel colours, vivid prints and relaxed
cuts—all beautifully feminine without
the slightest touch of cutesiness.

Gothersgade 58, 1123 København K
www.stinegoya.com

3 Le Beau Marché

Antiques, old maps and boxes and boxes of good wine: Le Beau Marché is all about the beautiful things in life. This is not the place to seek Scandinavian minimalism; rather, the store brims with designer items, furniture and decorative objects sourced from around the globe. It also stocks a great selection of French wines, which are available for tasting in the relaxed wine bar at the rear of the building.

Ny Østergade 32, 1101 København K
www.beaumarche.dk

10

Sandy, Nikolaj Plads

ATELIER SEPTE

4 Atelier September

This café's previous life as an antiques store is reflected everywhere in the details of its interiors. Atelier September has become a favourite meeting place for Copenhagen's young urban crowd and the city's fashion scene, who come here for the friendly, relaxed atmosphere. The most popular item on the menu is the delicious rye bread with avocado, chives and chilli for €10—a little luxury that's well worth it!

Gothersgade 30, 1123 København K
www.atelierseptember.dk

5 Tage Andersen

From outside, Tage Andersen could be mistaken for an ordinary florist's shop, but nothing could be further from the truth! It's rather a store, gallery, source of inspiration and museum all in one, so be prepared to pay a few krones admission if you don't buy anything. Allow yourself to be astonished by its opulent floral arrangements and Baroque still lifes tucked away in various nooks, and don't be surprised if you see a peacock parading across the courtyard.

Ny Adelgade 20, 1104 København K
www.tage-andersen.com

6 Generator Hostel

The Generator Hostel is an affordable insider tip: its location right in the heart of the city is simply unbeatable, as are its rates. If you don't like dormitories, there's also a choice of twin, double and triple rooms, which are small but very functional and have their private bathrooms. Don't miss the first-floor lounge, which even locals visit for its live music and inexpensive drinks and snacks.

Adelgade 5, 1304 København K
www.generatorhostels.com

7 Llama

The Cofoco Group runs some of Copenhagen's best and most popular restaurants, with fantastic food at inexpensive prices, including the very charming Llama. No wonder this place has quickly gained a dedicated following among the city's food aficionados: its colourful dishes offer a selection of the very best Latin American cuisine has to offer, from Peru to Bolivia, from Ecuador to Chile and Mexico. Mains are from around €15.

Lille Kongensgade 14, 1074 København K
www.llamarestaurant.dk

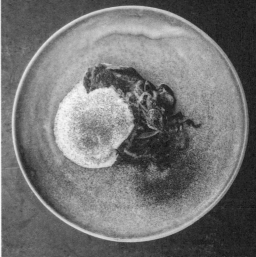

Bobby, Silkegade

8 Magasin

Magasin is Copenhagen's most upmarket department store. Opened in 1870 and located directly opposite the Danish State Opera, it exudes an air of nineteenth-century elegance on the outside, while its interiors couldn't be more up-to-date. Its seven levels are stocked with exclusive brands of cosmetics, home accessories and fashion. Visit the basement for the city's most eclectic food department or to take a break in one of the restaurants and cafés.

Kongens Nytorv 13, 1095 København K
www.magasin.dk

9 Birger Christensen

The city's most exclusive fashion store is right in the middle of Copenhagen's main shopping mile, the Strøget. Birger Christensen sells fashion, shoes and accessories by big international labels. Browse the shelves for designs by Yves Saint Laurent, Prada, Hermès and Dolce & Gabbana, plus fur coats made in Denmark. Birger Christensen is the city's only fashion boutique to stock Chanel.

Østergade 38, 1100 København K
www.birger-christensen.com

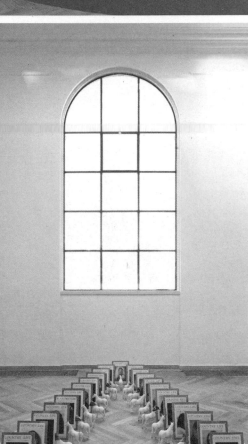

10 Kunsthal Charlottenborg

This gallery, housed in the Danish Royal Family's former town palace, has one of Europe's largest collections of contemporary art and is home to the Royal Danish Academy of Fine Arts. Its exhibitions, which change three times a year, cover a very broad spectrum, with the gallery's programme ranging from retrospectives of established Danish artists to showcases of up-and-coming international artists.

Kongens Nytorv 1, 1051 København K
www.kunsthalcharlottenborg.dk

11 Jane Kønig

Jane Kønig, one of Denmark's most popular jewellery designers, sells her intricate designs in a tiny shop right next to her studio. One of the main inspirations Kønig explores is the interplay between old and new, for example through combining classic gemstones with modern materials. Her 'love tags' make very popular souvenirs: these small, round pendants are stamped with customised initials.

Gothersgade 54, 1123 København K
www.janekoenig.dk

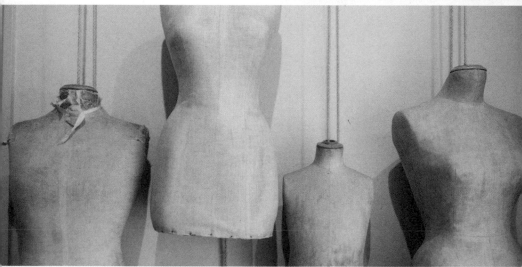

12 The Standard

Claus Meyer's presence in Copenhagen is unmissable. Meyer, co-owner of the world-renowned Michelin star-rated restaurant noma, has recently branched out into delis, bakeries and even cooking classes. His most recent venture, The Standard, is a jazz club in a waterfront 1937 art deco building. Behind the light green façade are a live music club, three restaurants and two bars. A simply fabulous place for food, drinks and music!

Havnegade 44, 1058 København K
www.thestandardcph.dk

13 Designmuseum Danmark

Denmark is synonymous with great design. This museum, dedicated to Danish and international design, is located in a splendid rococo building that was once Denmark's first public hospital. In the warmer months the café spills out into the lovely garden, which also serves as a performance space. The museum shop has a great selection of design and craft books and gifts.

Bredgade 68, 1260 København K
designmuseum.dk

14 Wood Wood

Wood Wood has become one of the flagships of Danish fashion. The label's first designs were pure streetwear for skaters, but it started broadening its range a few years ago and now includes not only hoodies, caps and backpacks, but also dresses, jackets and shirts. The store also stocks a selection of on-trend labels such as Barbour, Band of Outsiders and Comme des Garçons.

Grønnegade 1, 1107 København K
www.woodwood.dk

15 Kaf Bar

This little café looks quite unassuming from the outside, which is good for us: if word got out just how comfy it is, it would soon be entirely impossible to grab one of its rather unconventional seats. Kaf Bar is already very popular, but worth a wait if you're after great coffee, delicious snacks made from organic ingredients or a selection of juices and teas. Kaf Bar is run by school buddies Rasmus Damsbo and Mikkel Bang.

Antonigade 9, 1106 København K

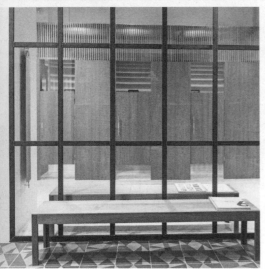

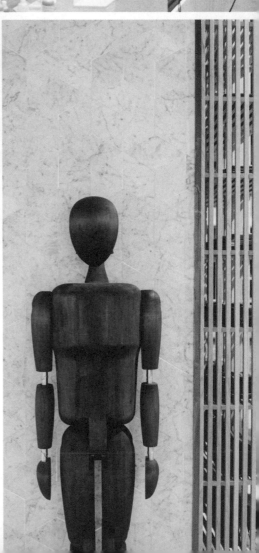

16 NN07

The initials in this Danish designer brand stand for 'No Nationality' to reflect a philosophy of freedom and a love of travel and adventure. But fear not—this menswear label is not about shrill outdoor clothing. Far from it. It's all about beautifully wearable basics and timeless shirts, pants and suits, plus a great range of denim. The NN07 flagship store is sumptuously styled with plenty of pale wood, white marble and patterned tiles.

Gammel Mønt 7, 1117 København K
www.nn07.com

17 Casa Shop

This place, one of Copenhagen's most popular furniture and designer stores, is 400 square metres of interiors heaven with great designs from all over the world. It stocks lamps and furniture from Italy and Spain, kitchens and bathroom furniture from Germany, and of course famous Danish classics, like Arne Jacobsen's 'Egg' and 'Swan' chairs. The smaller items make excellent souvenirs, and the knowledgeable staff are always happy to help.

Store Regnegade 2, 1110 København K
www.casashop.dk

18 Rue Verte

If this place seems a little dim and full of nooks and crannies, don't be too surprised: the building is more than 250 years old. There seems to be room after room behind every corner, making browsing through Rue Verte seem almost like exploring somebody's apartment, only you're allowed to touch everything. Come here for luscious velvet, opulent patterns and ornate candelabra. It'd only be kitsch if the owners didn't have such impeccable taste.

Ny Østergade 11, 1101 København K

www.rueverte.dk

19 Ganni

Fashion label Ganni has been designing
women's fashion since 2000 and has
already gathered a dedicated following.
Its shop on Store Regnegade was the first
of the label's fourteen flagship stores, now
located in Denmark, Norway, Germany and
the UK. The collection is displayed between
palm trees and cacti, and complemented
by lingerie, shoes and accessories. Ganni
fashion is colourful, youthful and often
inspired by vintage classics.

Store Regnegade 12, 1110 København K
www.ganni.com

Casper, Kronprinsensgade

20 Storm

Storm is all about bringing a range of labels together in the one concept store. The focus is on exclusive items by international brands with a somewhat extravagant touch, but aimed at a young clientele. Find handbags and clothes by French labels including Céline and Saint Laurent next to cool streetwear by Pigalle, Wood Wood and Supreme. There's even a small book section with an excellent selection of design and art books and trendy magazines.

Store Regnegade 1, 1110 København K
www.stormfashion.dk

21 Ørgreen Optics

The eyewear label Ørgreen—famous
for its colourful frames—designs all of
its pieces in Denmark and then has them
handmade in Japan. Its 150-square-metre
flagship store could almost be taken for
an art gallery, with its grey stone staircases,
wooden sculptures and light installations.
Ørgreen stocks a large selection of not only
its own designs, but also eyewear by Reiz,
Blinde, Zuerihorn and Ic! Berlin.

Store Regnegade 1, 1110 København K
www.orgreenoptics.com

22 Bering House of Flowers

Eric Bering opened his House of Flowers in 1972 and has since become one of Scandinavia's best-known florists. House of Flowers is now run by Eric's successor, Bjarne, but the philosophy has remained the same. The shop continues to specialise in lavish, rococo-inspired bouquets that are so impressive that Bering has been the Danish Royal Court's official purveyor of flowers for many years.

Landemærket 12, 1119 København K
www.beringflowers.com/en

23 *HAN Kjøbenhavn*

The label HAN Kjøbenhavn started out as an eyewear manufacturer, but has evolved into a truly great menswear label that has been showcased in international fashion magazines. This is the place to go for classic cuts and shapes, a wide selection of denim and great knitted jumpers. HAN is one of Copenhagen's best-designed stores and the only one in Denmark to stock the exclusive Le Labo scents—which make expensive, but classy, souvenirs or gifts.
Vognmagergade 7, 1120 København K
www.hankjobenhavn.com

24 Baum und Pferdgarten

While the name may sound German, Baum und Pferdgarten, founded in 1999 by friends Rikke Baumgarten and Helle Hestehave, is a Danish label through and through. Its flagship store is an expression of what the two designers are all about: contrasts and the interplay between feminine and masculine elements, tough fabrics and delicate silks. The lounge is so comfortable that it can sometimes be a real challenge to leave.

Vognmagergade 2, 1120 København K
www.baumundpferdgarten.dk

Ninna, Absalonsgade

25 DØP—The Organic Hot Dog Stand

You'll find hot dogs on every other corner in Copenhagen—they are Denmark's unofficial national food. But the city's best hot dogs are found right here, at DØP. The sausages are organic, and the wholemeal rolls homemade. 'Fransk Hot Dogs' (French hot dogs), rolls stuffed with sausage and a special sauce, are firm local favourites.

Købmagergade, near the round tower
1150 København K
www.døp.dk/da/om-doep

26 Time's Up Vintage

If you like second-hand, yet classy fashion, then make sure you don't miss Time's Up Vintage. This friendly basement store stocks a lot of fashion treasures, including vintage Chanel handbags, Hermès scarves in any imaginable colour and historic designer items. The pieces are not cheap, but they're all investments in timeless classics that you won't find anybody else wearing. Time's Up Vintage also has great men's fashion.

Krystalgade 4, 1172 København K
www.timesupshop.com

27 Henrik Vibskov

Henrik Vibskov is without doubt one of the
biggest names in Danish fashion design.
Vibskov, an artist and fashion designer,
is renowned for creating a very diverse
range of fashion without ever abandoning
his avant-garde roots. Visit his flagship
store for colourful knits and extravagant
cuts, plus relatively inexpensive
accessories, such as laptop sleeves and
socks. He also stocks some high fashion
labels, including Yoshi Yamamoto.
Krystalgade 6, 1172 København K
www.henrikvibskovboutique.com

28 Democratic Coffee Bar

A book and a great cup of coffee is always an excellent match, and this is pretty much what the Democratic Coffee Bar in Copenhagen's city library is all about. Owner Oliver Oxfeldt serves some of the city's best coffee right next to the library entrance, and you can perfect the experience with baked-on-the-premises croissants, panini, cakes and waffles. A tall bookshelf next to the door is extensively stocked with magazines and art books for leisurely browsing.

Krystalgade 15, 1172 København K

29 Wardrobe 19

Shoes stacked in bookshelves, jackets hanging from pipes, and a vintage telephone beneath the hat rack—Wardrobe 19 cultivates a very idiosyncratic look and stocks clothes for men who are comfortable with their sense of fashion. It's called 'heritage look' and means unbleached denim, check shirts and jackets that wouldn't look out of place on grandad, as well as a range of great boots, leather shoes and travel bags. And moustache wax, of course.

Larsbjørnsstræde 19, 1454 København K
www.wardrobe19.com

The Royal Guard watching over Amalienborg Palace

30 Project 4

While the guys browse Wardrobe 19, the girls can head to Project 4 next door. This shop stocks a fabulous selection of relaxed fashion by various labels, but its main attraction would be its amazing— and amazingly inexpensive—range of accessories: shoes, handbags and purses made of exquisitely soft leather, designed by small labels. At Project 4 you'll also find a small collection of jewellery made by some of the best local designers.

Larsbjørnsstræde 19, 1454 København K
www.project4.dk

31 Summerbird

Simply the city's best chocolate! Every Copenhagener shops at this chocolaterie sooner or later, and Summerbird is rightly famous for its sweet little works of art for all occasions, from birthday almonds through to miniature concoctions to sweeten the first day at school. Visitors should not miss the flødeboller, chocolate marshmallows with deliciously flavoured fillings—try the one with liquorice. Oh, and get some chocolate almonds to nibble on.

Ny Østergade 9, 1101 København K
www.summerbird.dk

32 Perch's

Except for the electrical lighting, everything in this tea shop is exactly the way it was when Perch's opened in 1835. The staff wear starched aprons, and tea is sold loose and weighed on mechanical scales. You can even buy a bag of Danish Queen Margarethe's favourite blend. If the store is too busy for your liking, walk around the corner and up the stairs: there's an amazing, beautifully old-fashioned tea salon on the first floor.

Kronprinsensgade 5, 1114 København K
www.perchs.dk

33 The Jane

At The Jane, stairs take you down into a netherworld that seems straight out of *Mad Men*. Expect dim lights, wide Chesterfield sofas and bookshelves full of musty old tomes. These hide secret doors that are opened on weekends to extend the space. The staff at this nightclub and bar are excellent and take the time to look after their customers. At any moment you expect to see Don Draper walk through the door.

Gråbrødretorv 8, 1154 København K
www.thejane.dk

34 Acne

The Pistol boots and Rita leather jackets by Swedish mega-label Acne are must-haves of street style. Acne operates three stores in Copenhagen; the largest and most beautiful, right in the centre, sells the label's womenswear and menswear collections in an environment that looks more like a club or art gallery than a shop. Even if you're not much into style, pick up a pair of Acne jeans, which are renowned for their great fit and virtually indestructible quality.

Pilestræde 40, 1112 København K
www.acnestudios.com/stores

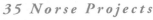

35 Norse Projects

Norse Projects is all about Scandinavian fashion for men. It's a small label that has gained a big following, especially for its caps and shirts, which are sold in the hippest of hip boutiques from Paris to New York. The Norse Projects flagship store stocks not only the label's own complete collection, but also limited-edition collaborations with other labels that can be difficult to find, plus an excellent selection of sneakers and bags.

Pilestræde 41, 1112 København K
www.norseprojects.com

36 Maria Black

Although Danish jewellery designer Maria Black has moved to London, she still feels very much connected to her home town of Copenhagen and has designed her store with a lot of loving attention. Its elegant wallpapers and display cases perfectly match her designs, which Maria herself has described as 'Lego for fashionistas'. The pieces can be combined and stacked in numerous ways to create ever-new looks and reflect different facets of a personality.

Silkegade 13, 1113 København K
www.maria-black.com

37 Illums Bolighus

This place right in the centre of Copenhagen is sheer heaven for fans of exquisite interiors. Illums Bolighus is much more than a furniture store: its range is so vast that it could almost be described as a museum of modern design. Come here for a who's who of the international designer scene, from classics including Eames and Arne Jacobsen through to contemporary Danish designers. The ground floor has small items that make great souvenirs.

Amagertorv 10, 1160 København K
www.illumsbolighus.dk

38 Illum

While Illums Bolighus is all about interiors, its big sister, the Illum department store, caters for everything else. This is a very elegant store with marble stairs connecting the various levels and a large number of very helpful and knowledgeable staff. It's a shoppers' paradise with an enormous selection of fashion labels. The cosmetics department on the ground floor, with its focus on natural products, is always worth a visit.

Østergade 52, 1100 København K
www.illum.dk

39 The Royal Café

The Royal Café is the birthplace of 'smushi'—Danish smørrebrød in practical sushi size, topped with fish, sliced meats or cheese. These delectable savoury bites are justly famous well beyond Copenhagen. This high-ceilinged café is furnished with classical pieces of Danish design by Fritz Hansen, Holmegaard and Bang & Olufsen; pastel colours and floral motifs on the walls give it a light and airy, almost girly, note.

Amagertorv 6, 1160 København K
www.royalsmushicafe.dk

40 HAY House

No self-respecting interiors magazine or blog, and certainly no hipster apartment, could be truly complete without the odd item by HAY. This Danish furniture and home furnishings company is what everybody who's anybody in the design world talks about, and its large flagship store shows why: great design and quality at (relatively) inexpensive prices. You enter HAY House via a lift, then stroll through its display area, which is laid out like an apartment.

Østergade 61, 1110 København K
www.hay.dk

41 Condesa

Condesa's mojo comes from delicious, fresh Mexican food such as tacos and ceviches paired with excellent cocktails. Many guests come mainly for its margaritas and palomas (you can also get pitchers of either—or both—for the table). This popular restaurant is run by the team that's also behind the renowned Dyrehaven restaurant in Vesterbro. On weekend nights, Condesa brings DJs in to spin some music.
Ved Stranden 18, 1061 København K
www.condesa.dk

42 Ruby

Ruby has everything you could possibly want in a cocktail bar. First you enter through an unassuming door without a sign, to set a mood of cool mystery. You then get a choice of sitting at the window or in the cosy basement, and the bar staff really know what they're doing. Ruby gets very busy late in the evening, so if you want the bartenders to take time to explain the drinks menu, it is best to come in the late afternoon.

Nybrogade 10, 1203 København K
www.ruby.dk

43 Pede & Stoffer Mens

Copenhagen has a few shops that clearly show that menswear stores need to be neither staid nor boring, and one of these is definitely Pede & Stoffer Mens. This is the place to go for a stylish, full range of menswear. Shop for a complete outfit and rest assured that it'll all end up looking just so. The Pede & Stoffer house brand features great shirts, jackets and denim, but the store also stocks other labels, including Wings + Horns (Canada) and Pendleton (USA).

Klosterstræde 15, 1157 København K
www.pedestoffer.com

44 La Glace

La Glace is Denmark's oldest and perhaps best café and patisserie, having sold exquisite pastries, cakes and coffee since 1870. As a family-run business that currently has the sixth generation of confectioners baking, it has maintained a perfect late-nineteenth-century ambience with plenty of brass, glass and mahogany. Tea, hot chocolate and coffee are served in bottomless pots that are refilled as often as you like. The cakes are out of this world!

Skoubogade 3–5, 1158 København K
www.laglace.dk

45 Greasy Spoon

The Greasy Spoon is a classic American diner in the middle of Copenhagen. The menu is as American as the restaurant's interior with its red vinyl-covered banquettes and an open kitchen. Come here not only for burgers, fried onion rings and chips, but also some classic American dishes that you don't often find on menus outside the US: pulled pork sandwiches, French toast or macaroni and cheese. Don't miss the milkshakes—they're the best in town!

Studiestræde 14, 1455 København K
www.greasyspoon.dk

WASTELAND

ATCHES 1=20 kr.
3=50 kr.

46 Wasteland

Leather jackets, lumberjack shirts, lace dresses from the 1980s, colourful cheerleader uniforms and everything else in second-hand American fashion are Wasteland's specialty. The shop has a plethora of more and less tasteful items from almost fifty years of American fashion history. It is best to set aside a bit of time for a visit; you're bound to find some treasures on its well-stocked hanging racks.

Studiestræde 19, 1455 København K
www.facebook.com/wastelandcopenhagen

47 Hotel Alexandra

Check in here for a bit of time travel: the hotel is completely fitted out with original designer items from the 1950s and 1960s. Each of the deluxe rooms and suites is dedicated to a star Danish designer and furnished with his or her pieces, so you have a choice of rooms in the style of Finn Juhl, Verner Panton, Hans J. Wegner or Arne Jacobsen. There are vinyl LPs and record players in the lobby and an excellent little library for the enjoyment of guests.

H. C. Andersens Blvd. 8, 1553 København V
www.hotelalexandra.dk

48 København K

Access this large second-hand shop through a gate leading into a courtyard. The store is well organised, and its wares are sorted by themes and colours, making browsing easy and fun. Large mirrors assist shoppers in deciding from among the huge selection of vintage shoes, jackets and other fashion items København K has to offer for both women and men. If you can't find anything here, just walk a few doors down the street to the second København K store.

Studiestræde 32, 1455 København K

49 Wood Wood Museum

Scandinavians seem to have a knack for outlet shopping, and this store is the perfect example. You won't find messy piles of clothing all over the place, and they won't all be in size XXS or XXL. Wood Wood is a popular Danish label, and its outlet store sells a large range of its own designs plus individual pieces from international labels such as Kenzo, Gitman or Opening Ceremony, reduced by up to 70 per cent.

Frederiksborggade 54, 1366 København K
www.woodwood.dk

50 Torvehallerne

Welcome to gourmet heaven! Torvehallerne
is a large covered market that you might
expect to find in southern Europe or perhaps
London, rather than in Copenhagen. There
are more than eighty merchants offering
their wares, from fresh fish from the Baltic
to cute cupcakes and innumerable local
specialties from all over Denmark, including
ox meat sausage and rhubarb juice from
Bornholm. Many of the stalls also sell
snacks and hot food.

Frederiksborggade 21, 1360 København K
www.torvehallernekbh.dk

51 Höst

With its minimalist furniture, roughly
plastered walls and rustic crockery, Höst
restaurant looks like a place straight out
of a Scandinavian interiors catalogue.
The carefully curated pieces combine very
effectively to create the ambience of a rural
farm right in the centre of Copenhagen.
Höst's master chefs focus on high-quality
local ingredients and simple dishes;
it is best to book a table online before
you arrive in Copenhagen.
Nørre Farimagsgade 41, 1364 København K
www.cofoco.dk/en/restaurants/hoest

52 SP34

While SP34 is a relatively new hotel, it has quickly become a firm favourite with guests who really value great design. Its look is very Scandinavian: practical and always simply beautiful. The generous rooms are full of natural light and feature extremely comfy beds. To top it off, SP34 is located very centrally, and has a daily 'wine hour' during which wine is on the house. Wi-Fi is free and fast, breakfast is organic and the price is right.

Jarmers Plads 3, 1453 København K
www.brochner-hotels.dk/our-hotels/sp34/

53 Ny Carlsberg Glyptotek

The Glyptotek, established by the founder of the Carlsberg brewery in 1888, houses a collection of antique art, including Roman, Etruscan and Greek artefacts, as well as nineteenth- and twentieth-century art. However, what makes this museum really special is the winter garden with its lovely, popular café. Sit among palm trees, ferns and marble statues, listen to the gently lapping fountain, and transport yourself to the tropics. Admission is free on Sundays.

Dantes Plads 7, 1556 København V
www.glyptoteket.dk

54 Toldboden

Toldboden, a former multi-purpose hall
that is now used for a wide range of events,
is next to Copenhagen's old citadel.
You don't have to rent the whole place,
though, to enjoy it: its Harbour Bar and Grill
are open throughout the summer, weather
permitting. The self-service restaurant
has delicious fish dishes, and Toldboden's
weekend brunch is rightly popular.
The bar is often used for live concerts.
Nordre Toldbod 24, 1259 København K
www.toldboden.com

JETTE
EGELUND

Danish design is world-famous for its timeless elegance, and Vipp, a furniture design company with a great knack for beautiful everyday objects, is one of the best-known Danish brands. Vipp is very much a family business. Jette Egelund, daughter of founder Holger Nielsen, tells us how a small metalwork shop became a global brand, what's special about Danish design, and where to find her favourite spots in Copenhagen.

Tell us something about the company's history.

I'm the daughter of Holger Nielsen, who founded the company. He established a small metalworking shop in 1931, after he'd come into a bit of money through sheer luck: he won a car in a competition, but sold it because he didn't have a driver's licence. He then spent the money on a metalworking lathe and established a small factory, next to which I grew up.

Vipp became world-famous with a rubbish bin. What's the story of that bin?

My mother had a small hairdresser's shop, and she asked my father to design and make a rubbish bin that she'd be able to open and close without using her hands. This is how the famous pedal bin was invented. My father, Holger, was no designer; he was a metal turner, and for him, good design always followed function. I wish that my father had lived to see how his pedal bin from his small Copenhagen workshop made it all the way to the New York MoMA. He'd be so proud!

How did the bin make its way from a hairdressing salon to MoMA?

That took a long time. My mother had a lot of doctors' and dentists' wives as customers, and they thought that the bin would be perfect for their husbands' practices. Which it was, but that meant that pedal bins were associated with medical and dental practices in Denmark—nobody wanted to have one at home. It took a lot of convincing for the bin to take off.

And how did you do that?

My father died in 1992, and my mother and I inherited his factory. I resigned from my job and learned how to operate the ancient factory machinery. At the time, Vipp only had a single employee, and he helped me operate these heavy monsters. I then travelled the world, from one furniture fair to the next to find customers, until finally some international designer companies saw how much potential was in the product. And as soon as international sales had taken off, the Danes started buying our bins too. My children have recently taken over running the company, so we're third-generation now.

But the Vipp Concept Store in central Copenhagen stocks a lot more than bins!

Of course! The pedal bins are our trademark, though. They are virtually unchanged from my father's original design, and we sell them in five sizes. However, we manufacture a lot more, including many products for bathrooms and kitchens, from towel rails to toothbrush cups. Our team also designs kitchens from scratch. We still use a lot of steel and rubber in our products, just like my father did, and everything we do is about smart design, high-quality materials and durability. I'm particularly proud of our small porcelain range, which Annemette Kissow makes exclusively for us.

*What is it that distinguishes
Danish design?*

Maybe it is what my father always put at the forefront of everything he did, the famous idea of 'form follows function'. That saying didn't originate in Denmark, but it summarises what we do. Design can make life both more beautiful and easier, and both are important.

*Will you tell us about your favourite
spots in Copenhagen?*

I love going out for dinner, and luckily Copenhagen has a large number of excellent restaurants. There's *Kiin Kiin* in Nørrebro, for example, the first Asian restaurant here to be awarded a Michelin star. I just love the aromas! I also often go to *Relæ* (p. 134), which does great food: traditional dishes, but with real refinement.

Which are your favourite stores?

I'm a great fan of Danish designs, including in fashion. Malene Birger is one of my favourites. I love browsing through *Magasin* (p. 29), but I also often stroll around the shops and boutiques around here, at Islands Brygge. And *Jane Kønig*'s jewellery is great, of course (p. 32).

What do you do in your spare time?

I work with my family, but I still love spending time with them outside work. I attend as many concerts as I can in the new Mogens Dahl Concert Hall directly next to our office. Some of my favourite activities are walking and cycling along the waterways, and Copenhagen has plenty of those! My favourite bicycling route goes around the harbour, along the Kalvebod Brygge to the new Cykelslangen, an amazing bridge just for cyclists. From there you have a fabulous view of the Royal Library in the 'Black Diamond'.

749.-

549.-

NYHAVN

KONGENS NYTROV **M**

Nyhavn

Holbergsgade

Holmens Kanal

Niels Juels Gade

Admiralgade

Vindebrogade

Havnegade

Bådsmandsstræde

8

Trangravsvej

7

5

Strandgade

Christianshavns Kanal

4

Børsgade

SLOTSHOLMEN

Slotsholmsgade

Christians Brygge

Knippels-

bro

Tøjhusgade

Strandgade

S. Wilders-gade

Overgaden Oven Vandet

9

Burmeistersg.

Danneskiold-Samsøes Allé

CHRISTIANIA

3

2

Sankt Annæ Gade

Bådsmandsstræde

6

1

Strandg.

Torvegade

Johan Semps Gade

Overgaden Neden Vandet

Overgaden Oven Vandet

Prinsesseg.

10

M CHRISTIANSHAVN ST

Langebrogade

Dronningensgade

KØBENHAVNS HAVNEBADE

11

Torvegade

Vermlandsgade

STADSGRAVEN

Ved Stadsgraven

Amager Boulevard

Amagerbrogade

Svinget

Njalsgade

Norgesgade

Amagerfælledvej

M ISLANDS BRYGGE ST

12

CHRISTIANSHAVN & ISLANDS BRYGGE

Christianshavn and Islands Brygge are directly on the water, and these two suburbs live at a much more leisurely pace than the busy city centre. Yet they couldn't be more different, even though they are right next to each other: while Christianshavn is incredibly charming, with old buildings, intricate canals and a number of world-class restaurants, Islands Brygge is like a contemporary playground designed by the world's top architects. Both suburbs are best explored on foot.

1 Munk

Here is a wonderful, small furniture store off the main shopping streets. Owner Hans Peter Munk always picks a perfectly matched selection from the vast pool of excellent Nordic design, including some renowned interiors brands such as Muuto, Frama and Noness. However, he also stocks a number of rarities that you won't find anywhere else in Copenhagen. The large selection of posters and prints alone makes a visit worthwhile!

Torvegade 25, 1400 København K
www.munkshop.dk

2 Eiffel Bar

The counter of the Eiffel Bar is lined with
the usual suspects, a group of Yahtzee-
playing students occupy the lounge and
a pensioner plays the poker machine—
and all are chain-smoking. By day, the
Eiffel Bar is a charming, old-style pub,
but its vibe changes altogether after dark:
in flood young, hip city slickers in search
of the authentic ambience of a typical
Copenhagen wine bar (and inexpensive
drinks). A truly unique experience!

Wildersgade 58, 1408 København K
www.eiffelbar.dk

3 Sweet Treat

Sweet Treat may look like just another friendly neighbourhood café, but it has fans all over Copenhagen. The main reason are the enticingly displayed sweet delicacies after which the café is named: madeleines, cookies and cakes, all homemade, of course, plus good coffee and hot chocolate. Sweet Treat is also very popular for breakfast. If you take a particular liking to an item of crockery or decor, just ask—many are for sale.

Sankt Annæ Gade 3A, 1416 København K
www.sweettreat.dk

4 Danish Architecture Centre

Danish architecture is internationally renowned, and many of the world's best-known architects and town planners come from Denmark. To find the pulsating heart of Denmark's design scene, visit the Danish Architecture Centre, which has regularly changing, very fine exhibitions on individual architects and design schools. The shop stocks the largest collection of architecture and design books in Scandinavia.

Strandgade 27B, 1401 København K
www.dac.dk

5 *noma*

Welcome to the world's best restaurant! noma has been awarded this title by the British Restaurant Magazine no less than four times since 2010, mainly because of chef René Redzepi's extraordinary skill. Redzepi sources the ingredients for his beautiful dishes from Iceland, the Faroe Islands, Greenland and, of course, Denmark, and is considered the founder of New Nordic Cuisine. If you intend to dine at noma, book your table months ahead!

Strandgade 93, 1401 København K
www.noma.dk

Løvstræde

6 Christiania

Christiania offers a unique lifestyle, which comes as no surprise, as this suburb is a 'free town' that declared its independence from Denmark in 1971. Legally the people of Christiania may be on shaky ground, but they have created a reality that is indeed very un-Danish, with chaotic noise, crooked, colourful houses and marijuana being sold (illegally) at stalls as if it was salad greens. Leave your camera and smartphone tucked away—there's absolutely no photography!

Bådsmandsstræde 43, 1407 København K
www.christiania.org

7 Den Plettede Gris

Fashion designer and artist Henrik Vibskov recently opened a café next to his studio right on the water. You can't possibly miss Den Plettede Gris ('the spotted pig'): with its bright colours, angled lines and intricate wood structures, it looks like one of Vibskov's popular designs. However, there's much more to it than mere cuteness—you'll find some of the city's best coffee here.

Trangravsvej 5, 1436 København K
www.henrikvibskov.com

Exciting architecture on the Islands Brygge shore

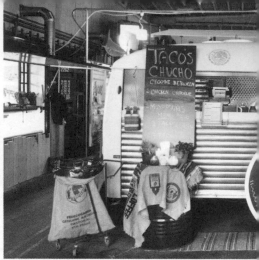

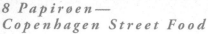

8 Papirøen—
Copenhagen Street Food

Two warehouses on the water at Papirøen—
Paper Island—are home to Copenhagen
Street Food, a place based on a simple but
ingenious concept: plenty of different food
carts and seating, plus great music. There
is a wide range of foods, from Mexican
tacos to Danish hot dogs, all freshly made
from local ingredients, and every stall serves
at least one dish for only 50 kroner.

Trangravsvej 14, Halle 7&8,
1436 København K
www.copenhagenstreetfood.dk

9 Parterre

This little café in an old building directly on Christianshavns Kanal has become a hot insider tip. While you need to walk down a few steps to enter, Parterre is anything but the dark theatrical space its name suggests; rather, it is a warm space full of natural light. The owners, a father-and-son team, serve breakfast, lunch and morning and afternoon teas. The coffee is from Swedish coffee roasters Koppi, and the menu is very reasonably priced.

Overgaden Oven Vandet 90,
1415 København K

10 Overgaden

This cultural centre, which was founded by a group of Danish artists in 1986, has established itself as an important centre for modern and experimental art. It stages acclaimed, frequently multi-disciplinary exhibitions ranging from classical paintings through to video installations, which are one of its specialties. Overgaden extends over two levels of a beautiful nineteenth-century building directly on the water.

Overgaden Neden Vandet 17,
1414 København K
www.overgaden.org

11 CPH Living

A lot of Copenhagen's charm is closely linked to the city's location on the water: ships, the sea and the harbour are a constant presence, but if that's still not quite maritime enough for you, book one of the twelve rooms in this converted cargo ship. CPH Living is moored on the shore of Islands Brygge, and each of its lovely rooms features large panoramic windows with views of the city and canal. The large sun deck is reserved for hotel guests.

Langebrogade 1C, 1411 København K
www.cphliving.com

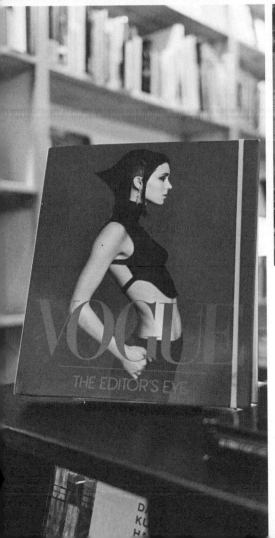

12 Kirkegaards Antikvariat

This small antiquarian bookshop in Islands Brygge specialises in photography, art and fashion books and also stocks rare tomes. Browse its shelves for high-brow treasures as well as pop culture. A narrow corridor leads to a rear section with an exhibition of particularly valuable items. Kirkegaards may be small, but it regularly organises concerts and temporary exhibitions. Check out the website for more information.

Islands Brygge 25, 2300 København S
www.kirkegaardsantikvariat.tumblr.com

KADEAU

MAGNUS HØEG KOFOED
& NICOLAI NØRREGAARD

In recent years, New Nordic Cuisine has conquered the international food world from its conceptual capital of Copenhagen. The fundamental idea is simple: cook only with local, seasonal ingredients. Among the star advocates of this philosophy are the people behind Kadeau, a Copenhagen restaurant right on the waterfront. Two of its owners tell us a little more about their concept.

What's the story behind Kadeau?

Nicolai Nørregaard: My business partners and I are just boys from Bornholm, a small island in the Baltic. We moved to Copenhagen, but always missed island life and above all the fresh produce, and so we decided to open a restaurant. We soon found a great building right on the beach—luckily before the global financial crisis, as we had to finance everything through loans. After that, things happened really quickly.

Magnus Høeg Kofoed: We had just about two weeks to renovate the place all over, by ourselves, with the help of more than thirty of our friends. At the time, we were not about gourmet cuisine, but simply about honest, good food.

And when did your food become first-class gastronomy?

M.H.K.: A year later, in 2008. noma had been hugely successful, but nobody outside René Redzepi's team cared at all about Nordic cuisine. We very much liked the approach of cooking with only local ingredients and restricted ourselves to an even narrower geography than others: our plan was to work exclusively with produce from Bornholm and Denmark.

N.N.: It was difficult, but inspirational.

Our self-imposed limitations really fired up my creativity. If I can only source carp, salmon, herring and mackerel from the Baltic, then I need to keep finding new ways to develop new dishes from these ingredients. We soon started exploring our local forests and meadows and built up relationships with local farmers.

And how did you turn your Bornholm restaurant into a Michelin-starred restaurant in Copenhagen?

N.N.: There were two reasons. Rasmus, my business partner, and I both had children in 2010, and our families live in Copenhagen. Also, our Bornholm restaurant is only open for a few months every year, as the island is very popular with tourists in summer, but pretty much deserted in winter. We wanted to be able to spend more time with our families and live on Bornholm for only three months in summer.

What makes Kadeau in Copenhagen special?

M.H.K.: Although our restaurant is right in the middle of Copenhagen, our roots are very clearly on Bornholm. When we cook, we always aim to recreate the wonderful flavours and aromas of our beloved island and to transport them to Copenhagen. While our city restaurant is very modern in style, we always want it to carry an island feeling, and that's what we are trying to do with all the fresh herbs, the ceramic tableware, local art and the general island flair.

How do you transport the flavours of Bornholm to Copenhagen?

N.N.: That's quite a challenge. Not so much because of the fresh produce, which we get delivered to the city, but seasonal produce is, of course, very limited during the winter months. So we gather whatever we can in summer and preserve everything we possibly can.

And in summer you close the Copenhagen restaurant and move your entire team to the island?

N.N.: Yes, exactly. Our whole restaurant moves to Bornholm for five weeks. We all live, cook and harvest together on an old farm.

You run not only the two Kadeau restaurants, but also the Pony restaurant in Vesterbro. What's the story with Pony?

M.H.K.: Pony is the cheeky little brother of Kadeau. It's a restaurant in Vesterbrogade, in the old premises of Kadeau, and it's all about a simpler version of our cooking. There's a small selection of à-la-carte dishes, and a four-course dinner that changes every day, which we call the 'Pony Kick'.

N.N.: All of the dishes are based on seasonal, local produce, and so Pony is very much part of the New Nordic movement, just like Kadeau. However, Pony focuses more on classic bistro cooking, using products from Bornholm and delicious foods from all over the rest of Denmark. We serve a selection of European wines made by winemakers who are very closely involved with their vineyards and whose roots go deep into their local regions.

M.H.K.: The premises are small, and the kitchen is small, but our passion for good food and wine is all the greater for it. We want our guests to enjoy a great evening without any fuss but with plenty of fantastic food and excellent wines to make it a truly memorable experience.

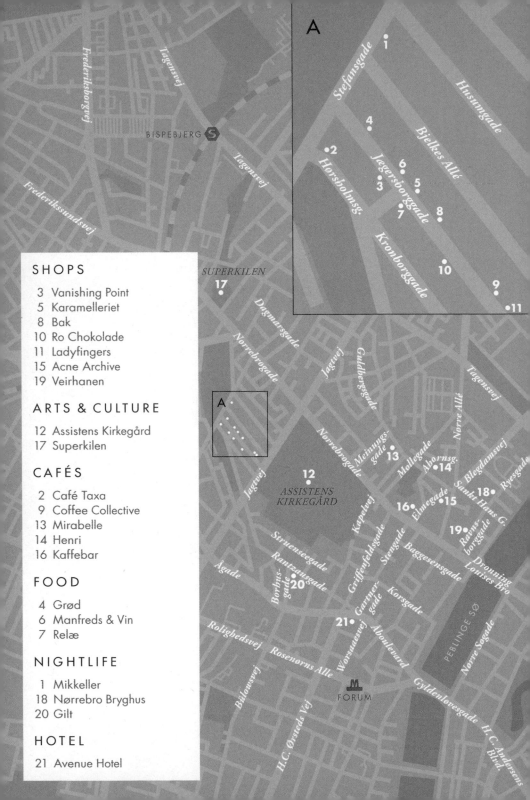

A

SHOPS

3 Vanishing Point
5 Karamelleriet
8 Bak
10 Ro Chokolade
11 Ladyfingers
15 Acne Archive
19 Veirhanen

ARTS & CULTURE

12 Assistens Kirkegård
17 Superkilen

CAFÉS

2 Café Taxa
9 Coffee Collective
13 Mirabelle
14 Henri
16 Kaffebar

FOOD

4 Grød
6 Manfreds & Vin
7 Relæ

NIGHTLIFE

1 Mikkeller
18 Nørrebro Bryghus
20 Gilt

HOTEL

21 Avenue Hotel

NØRREBRO

Nørrebro is a little chaotic, creative and multicultural. In this former working-class suburb west of the city, you'll find vegan snack bars next to tiny vintage fashion shops, kebab stands and hairdressers' shops. In the daytime, everybody is out and about in the cafés, parks and shops, but after dark it's all about a young crowd of students and creative people descending on the many bars and clubs to have a good time. Nørrebro showcases yet another face of Copenhagen: more colourful, less organised and orderly, but very, very likeable.

UNE 2011	50	31	MIKKELLER/ TO ØL	BETELGEUZE 5.5%	40
E 9.9 %	35	32	TO ØL/ MIKKELLER	OV-RAL 10.5%	40
BAR AMBIC 7%	35	33	MIKKELLER	IT'S ALIVE BA 8% CHARDONNAY MANGO	45

1 Mikkeller

Mikkel Borg Bjergsø was once a maths and physics teacher in Copenhagen who taught two of his students how to brew beer after school. The students were so successful that they established their own boutique brewery and went into partnership with their former teacher to found Mikkeller, which now runs bars all over the world, although the most beautiful one may still very well be in Nørrebro. There's a selection of forty beers on tap, which changes every month.
Stefansgade 35, 2200 København N
www.mikkeller.dk

TO ØL ⁵ᵗ	BA SNOWBALL	40			
TO ØL ⁷⁷	BA SANS FRONTIER	40	39	MIKKELLER ⁷·⁷ SPO
TO ØL	BA MINE IS BIGGER THAN YOURS 12.5% MUSCATE	45	40	MIKKELLER ⁷·⁷ SPO ELD

127

2 Café Taxa

Café Taxa is a true neighbourhood hub. There's always something happening in this large, rambling space: students share a table while studying for exams, young parents drop in with their kids and freelancers work at their laptops to escape home for a few hours. Taxa serves inexpensive, freshly prepared food all day, and when the sun is out, the large outdoor area directly next to the Nørrebropark is perfect for soaking up a few rays.

Hørsholmsgade 32, 2200 København N
www.cafetaxa.dk

3 Vanishing Point

Jægersborggade is one of Copenhagen's most popular streets, especially among young creative people. The road is lined with many small, independent businesses, so it's wise to set aside a few hours for a leisurely stroll, even though Jægersborggade is just a few hundred metres long. Vanishing Point is Norwegian artist Sigrid Astrup's studio and shop—highly recommended for her quirky creations made of ceramic, wool and paper.

Jægersborggade 45, 2200 København N
www.vanishing-point.dk

4 Grød

Copenhageners love healthy food, and you'll find many restaurants and supermarkets offering a wide range of organic products. One of them is Grød: its name means 'porridge', and that's exactly what the two owners, Martin Daniali and Lasse Skjønning Andersen, specialise in. Tuck into spelt porridge with chestnut cream, apple and roasted almonds, for example, for a healthy start that will make you feel energised throughout the day.
Jægersborggade 50, 2200 København N
www.grød.com

5 Karamelleriet

Chocolate, toffee, fudge, sweet and salty liquorice—Karamelleriet produces sweets in every flavour imaginable. All of its irresistible confectionery is made and sold in this basement shop: you will be drawn inside by the delicious smell of homemade sweets wafting into the street. Karamelleriet sells beautifully packaged gift boxes, but you can also make your own selection from the wooden bulk containers, so nobody has to miss out on their personal favourites.

Jægersborggade 36, 2200 København N
www.karamelleriet.com

6 Manfreds & Vin

Good food plays an important role in Copenhagen, as is obvious from the many gourmet and Michelin-starred restaurants, but visits to these lofty establishments are usually reserved for very special occasions. That's why some of Copenhagen's star chefs also run more down-to-earth, less expensive restaurants, and Manfreds & Vin is one of them. It is owned by the same people as Relæ across the road and has a good selection of organic wines.

Jægersborggade 40, 2200 København N
www.manfreds.dk

Rie, Istedgade

7 Relæ

Chef Christian Puglisi's restaurant may be the least pretentious of Copenhagen's Michelin-starred restaurants. Puglisi, a Danish chef with an Italian background, cooks exquisite, internationally renowned food, yet the atmosphere at Relæ is always relaxed and welcoming. That may be why many of Copenhagen's famous chefs call it their personal favourite for dining out. Be sure to book a table well ahead!

Jægersborggade 41, 2200 København N
www.restaurant-relae.dk

8 Bak

This store is a marvellous collection of lovely things. The shelves are stacked with candles, glassware and ceramics, and dotted between them are cacti and succulents. A few select, expertly renovated pieces of vintage furniture and an exquisite selection of magazines and stationery perfectly complement the ambience.

Bak is retail paradise for customers who love beautiful everyday objects, and it doesn't even seem to matter that the store has no sign on its door.

Jægersborggade 30, 2200 København N

9 Coffee Collective

The Coffee Collective, a micro-roasting business that really introduced Copenhagen to good coffee, is synonymous with the art of coffee roasting all over the world. It has three cafés around Copenhagen that are always busy. The one in Jægersborggade has very few seats, so most customers get their flat whites or short blacks to take away. The Coffee Collective baristas really are as good as one would expect, and are always happy to help you choose.

Jægersborggade 10, 2200 København N
www.coffeecollective.dk

Nougat peanut

Ingefær ganache

Hindbær ganache

Champagne ganache

Baileys ganache

Hyldeblomst fondant

Marcipan æble&kanel

Marcipan pistacie

ro chokolade
Handmade

VARM CHOKOLADE

10 Ro Chokolade

Yet another tiny, but impressive store. The chocolates are handmade in the small workshop behind the store. The owners place great value on working only with the very best ingredients for their exquisite creations, including genuine champagne, organic honey and high-quality chocolate from all over the world. Ro is worth a visit at any time of the year: in summer for its homemade ice cream, and in winter for simply the best hot chocolate.

Jægersborggade 25, 2200 København N
www.ro-chokolade.com

Colourful signs on Jægersborggade point to the best shops.

11 *Ladyfingers*

This store is the result of six jewellery designers getting together to sell their pieces, and what a result it is—a woman's dream come true. While each of the six artists has her own personal style and approach, their idiosyncratic creations combine into a beautiful whole. Ladyfingers jewellery is delicate, minimalistic and strongly geometric, yet very feminine at the same time. And the inexpensive prices are particularly attractive.

Jægersborggade 4, 2200 København N
www.lady-fingers.dk

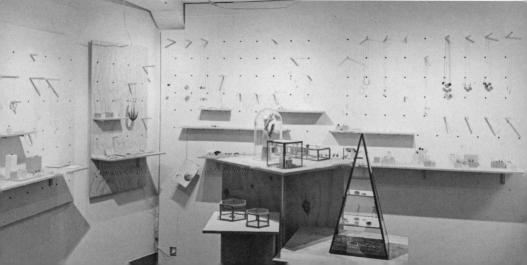

DIGTEREN

HANS CHRISTIAN

ANDERSEN

F. 2DEN APRIL 1805

D. 4DE AUGUST 1875

DEN SJÆL GUD I SIT BILLEDE HAR SKABT

ER UFORKRÆNKELIG, KAN EI GAAE TABT

VORT JORDLIV HER ER EVIGHEDENS FRØ

VORT LEGEM DØER, MEN SJÆLEN KAN EI DØE

H. C. A.

12 Assistens Kirkegård

No matter how busy and noisy the city may be, there always seems to be heavenly peace under the tall trees of Assistens Kirkegård. This cemetery is the last resting place of many famous people, including the Danish national hero Hans Christian Andersen, philosopher Søren Kierkegaard and a few renowned American jazz musicians who lived in Copenhagen in the 1950s and 1960s, such as Ben Webster and Kenny Drew.

Kapelvej 4, 2200 København N
www.assistens-kirkegaard.dk

13 Mirabelle

Boutique bakeries are the latest thing in Copenhagen: many of them work with organic ingredients and operate their own, local bakehouses. One of them is Mirabelle in Kapelvej, which is run by Christian Puglisi, owner of Relæ and former chef at noma. Mirabelle shares a building with Puglisi's new pizzeria, Baest, and that's why you get fabulous pizza here in the afternoons, plus great sweet things and, of course, excellent Danish bread.

Guldbergsgade 29, 2200 København N

14 Henri

The helically striped pole in the shop window gives Henri away as a classic barber's shop. Everything inside the stylishly unrendered brick walls is genuinely American vintage, from the barber chairs to the music and pomade. The seventy-year-old master barber comes in only once a week, but his young colleagues cut and shave every day. Henri doesn't cater for women's haircuts, but there is a comfortable café at the front of the shop, where anyone can sit and relax.

Ahornsgade 25, 2200 København N

15 Acne Archive

Acne Archive is at one end of Elmegade.
This narrow little store is a hot insider tip
among fashion fans and definitely worth
a visit, as it is where the Swedish luxury
label sells individual items and clothes from
past collections for a fraction of the often
very high original retail price. Acne Archive
stocks both women's and men's fashion,
plus shoes and bags. Walk through to the
rear for a large selection of Acne denim.
Elmegade 21, 2200 København N
www.acnestudios.com

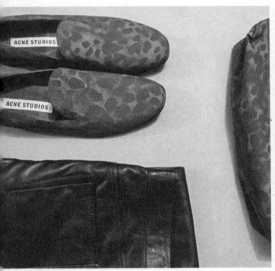

16 Kaffebar

This popular café seems to change its name quite regularly, but not its delightful nature. Come here for excellent coffee and a relaxed atmosphere. When the sun is out, sit outside at one of the shared tables on the pavement, where most of the customers seem to congregate. Kaffebar serves a simple, but yummy and inexpensive breakfast, and warm panini for lunch. There are also freshly squeezed juices and a small selection of good wines on the menu.

Elmegade 4, 2200 København N
www.elmegade4.dk

17 Superkilen

This park is divided into three sections: red, green and black. Superkilen is a huge playground for adults, adorned with larger-than-life objects from all over the world. The suburb of Nørrebro is home to people from more than fifty countries, and some of the locals were invited to choose typical objects from their home countries for the park. Look closely, and you may discover a donut sign from Tennessee, the famous Osborne bull from southern Spain and benches from Brazil.

Nørrebrogade 210, 2200 København N

18 Nørrebro Bryghus

The Nørrebro Bryghus is where award-winning brewer Anders Kissmeyer and his team work their magic. The brewing happens in the rear of the building, where up to ten different beers are produced on any given day. The basement bar and first-floor restaurant are where you get to taste the fruits of Anders' efforts. The menu features hearty Danish home cooking that goes perfectly with the beers; or you can just buy some of the colourfully bottled beers.

Ryesgade 3, 2200 København N
www.noerrebrobryghus.dk

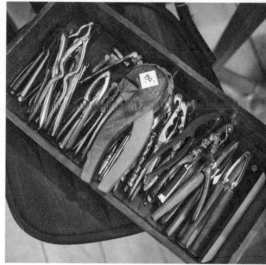

19 Veirhanen

Ravnsborggade seems to be just a long line of antiques and second-hand stores—this street is Copenhagen's best-known treasure trove. One of these stores is Veirhanen, which strains at the seams with old crockery, lamps, chairs, dressers and interior decorations. Owner Niels Tryde also has a whole warehouse full of furniture outside the city, so if you're after something specific, make sure you ask.

Ravnsborggade 12, 2200 København N
www.veirhanen.dk

20 Gilt

It's not only star chefs who are into the New Nordic movement: the bar staff at Gilt are just as enthusiastic about local, Nordic products and almost-forgotten flavours. Owner Peter Altenburg has mixed drinks for twenty years, and works mainly with typically Scandinavian ingredients such as rhubarb, elderflower and sea buckthorn. The bar is hidden behind an unassuming door, but step in to find a rather refined ambience with plenty of wood and deep leather seats.

Rantzausgade 39, 2200 København N
www.gilt.dk

21 Avenue Hotel

This award-winning boutique hotel is ideally located right between Frederiksberg and Nørrebro and therefore great for exploring both of these suburbs and the city. The nineteenth-century building was designed by the same architect who did the grandiose entrance to the famous Tivoli Gardens amusement park. The rooms are modern and comfortable, Wi-Fi is free throughout the hotel and there's a lovely open fireplace in the courtyard.

Åboulevard 29, 1960 Frederiksberg C
www.avenuehotel.dk

TIKKIE
OESTRICH
IVERSEN

Tikkie Oestrich Iversen, aka Adelié, is one of Denmark's most popular fashion bloggers. A few years ago, she opened her own store on Guldbergsgade in Nørrebro, where she shares with her customers her fantastic sense of style and pieces by her favourite (often Danish) designers, including Stine Goya, Peter Jensen and Libertine-Libertine. She explains to us what makes Danish style and Nørrebro so special.

Who is Adelié?
Adelié is my alter ego, my fashion personality. And, of course, the store in which we are right now.

Tell us a bit about Adelié.
Adelié started as the fashion blog *adelie.dk*. I blogged about up-and-coming fashion trends and labels I liked, and I showed my outfits on a daily basis. I soon had quite a large, dedicated following and the positive feedback encouraged me to open my own online store, where I sold pieces I liked to wear myself. Blogging is international, and I loved the thought that readers from all over the world would be able to buy from me.

Yet you ultimately opened a brick-and-mortar store on Guldbergsgade. How did that come about?
Many of my customers wanted to try on clothes before buying them from me, and obviously they couldn't do that in my flat. When this small store in my neighbourhood became vacant a few years ago, I jumped at the opportunity and opened a proper shop, which now complements my little Adelié universe.

So you live in Nørrebro?
Yes, I love Nørrebro and live right on the lakes, only about five minutes' walk from the shop. That's why I know this suburb well, and I always thought that it needed a proper fashion store. Before I opened Adelié, people went to the city or to Vesterbro to find all the labels I now sell here. I recognised that as a clear niche that I'd be able to fill. Before, you could only find streetwear or second-hand clothes locally.

What do you like about this suburb?
Nørrebro really feels like a village, in the best sense. People go to the city to work, and it feels busy and hectic. Vesterbro is where Copenhageners go out, so it's also pretty fast-paced. Nørrebro is a little slower; there's a lot of green space, fresh air and lots of light. That's what I love.

How would you describe Copenhagen women's sense of style?
Copenhagen style is casual and creative. We love mixing and matching different styles. You'll see, for example, women combining pretty, feminine pieces with typically male accessories such as sneakers and wide cuts. This keeps it interesting and makes sure it never looks just cute. This contrast has virtually become a trademark of Danish style in the fashion scene. At the moment, the entire scene is talking about 'normcore' as the latest trend, that is, more and more fashionistas wearing totally normal clothes, but making a statement with that. People in Denmark have done that for years. In Denmark, it's always been ok to wear sneakers out and about, and this has recently also cropped up in Paris and Milan.

Why is it that Danes seem to have such impeccable taste?
That's a good question! I think that design forms part of our Scandinavian DNA. We don't have a lot of local industry; instead,

we look for smart solutions for all sorts of problems. We are a small country that has gained international attention through good design, and that's something that is reflected in our everyday lives: in the way we furnish our homes and spaces, and how we dress. And ultimately we're simply very Scandinavian: unpretentious, practical and exquisite at second glance.

Who does the best breakfast in Nørrebro?

If Danes don't have much time for breakfast, they'll just have a cheese sandwich or roll. If I was after such a quick bite and a great coffee, I'd go to *Kaffeplantagen* at Sankt Hans Torv. At *Kaffebar* (p. 147) on Elmegade I often order scrambled eggs on rye bread. Both of these coffee places are unpretentious and very comfortable. I only discovered *Mirabelle* bakery (p. 142) quite recently. They do a fantastic sourdough bread!

And what are your favourite restaurants in the neighbourhood?

A number of restaurants have recently opened along the water, near where I live. There's *Gran Torino*, for example, a great pizzeria in a lovely space with inexpensive wine. I also love *20a* on Ravnsborggade, a tapas restaurant where I usually just order the dish of the day—you can trust them that it'll be really good. If I'm after something special, I'll go to *Manfreds & Vin* (p. 132) or *Relæ* (p. 134).

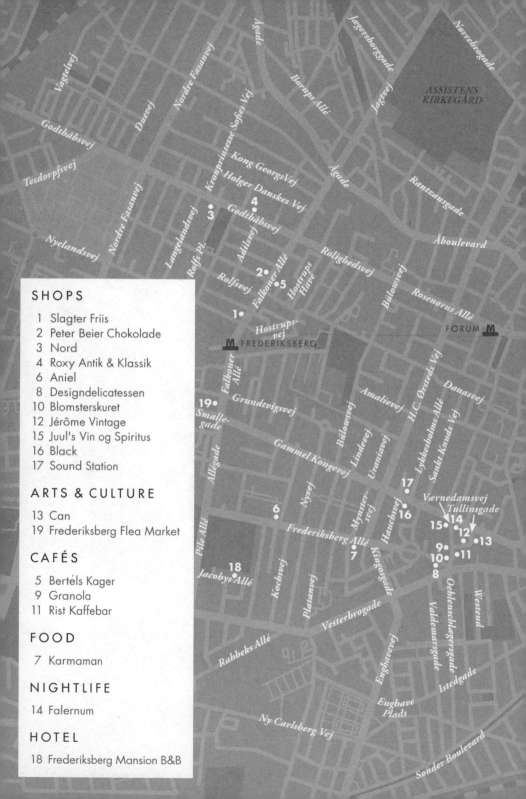

SHOPS

1 Slagter Friis
2 Peter Beier Chokolade
3 Nord
4 Roxy Antik & Klassik
6 Aniel
8 Designdelicatessen
10 Blomsterskuret
12 Jérôme Vintage
15 Juul's Vin og Spiritus
16 Black
17 Sound Station

ARTS & CULTURE

13 Can
19 Frederiksberg Flea Market

CAFÉS

5 Bertéls Kager
9 Granola
11 Rist Kaffebar

FOOD

7 Karmaman

NIGHTLIFE

14 Falernum

HOTEL

18 Frederiksberg Mansion B&B

FREDERIKSBERG

Frederiksberg is an upmarket suburb with wide boulevards, magnificent buildings and well-kept parks. It is also home to a number of embassies, but that doesn't mean that this suburb in Copenhagen's west is boring! Frederiksberg is rather a suburb for connoisseurs who want to enjoy the good life at a leisurely pace. There are exclusive boutiques and antiques stores next to cosy cafés and restaurants, trendy yoga studios and lovely delis. And sometimes, when the busy nightlife of colourful Vesterbro spills over onto the streets of Frederiksberg, it can even get boisterous!

1 *Slagter Friis*

Not many tourists explore Falkoner Allé in Frederiksberg, which is why it is an excellent place to get a taste of everyday life in Copenhagen. This street has a number of great delicatessens, all of which seem to have a dedicated clientele. Slagter Friis, a butcher's shop that has been run by the same family for five generations, is among them. Well worth a visit for the many Danish specialties it stocks alone.

Falkoner Allé 27, 2000 Frederiksberg
www.slagterfriis.dk

SAAZ BLONDE
ØL
TRØFFEL

PETER BEIER
CHOKOLADE

2 Peter Beier Chokolade

Danish chocolatier Peter Beier has set himself an ambitious goal: to make the world's best chocolate. He even bought his own cocoa plantation in the Caribbean, where he grows exactly the cocoa beans he wants. Ultimately, it's probably a matter of taste whether he sells the world's best chocolate or not, but his exquisite creations are definitely incredibly delicious. The gift boxes are quite expensive, but you can also buy individual chocolates.

Falkoner Allé 43, 2000 Frederiksberg
www.pbchokolade.dk

3 Nord

The name already gives away what this furniture store is all about: the designer pieces you'll find here are all Scandinavian-inspired, and most of the range consists of Danish brands, including HAY, Vipp and Muuto. Nord presents itself as a likeable local interiors specialist with a selection that is very much down to earth: look for colourful cushions, practical storage solutions, lots of great children's furniture and delightful toys.

Godthåbsvej 35, 2000 Frederiksberg
www.nordcopenhagen.dk

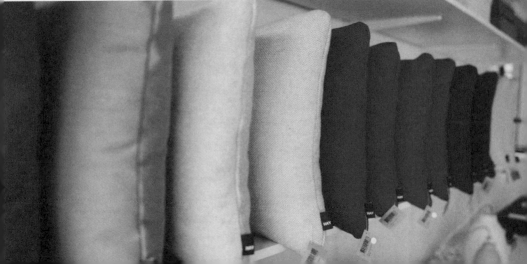

4 Roxy Antik & Klassik

This is another furniture store—or rather two separate, but interconnected stores—but not one that subscribes to Scandinavian minimalism. Its concept is instead to sell exquisite design pieces from the last century. Roxy Antik specialises in pieces dating from the first half of the twentieth century, while Roxy Klassik focuses on design classics from about the 1950s onwards, including such greats as Verner Panton, Charles and Ray Eames and Poul Henningsen.

Godthåbsvej 20, 2000 Frederiksberg
www.roxyantik.dk

5 Bertels Kager

Welcome to cheesecake paradise! The Bertels Kager café in Frederiksberg and its sister café in the city regularly score awards for their contemporary interpretations of New York cheesecake. Visit to admire their huge, handmade, heavenly cakes, which come in every conceivable variety: classic or with liquorice, Oreo cookies, fresh berries or caramel, among others. Enjoy your slice of cake with your favourite tea from a very extensive tea menu.

Falkoner Allé 54, 2200 Frederiksberg
www.bertelskager.dk

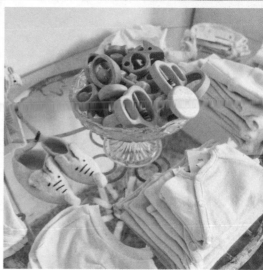

6 Aniel

Many Danes like organic products, and not just food: for some time there has been a strong trend towards children's clothes and toys made from natural materials. Aniel is a small shop that sells only organic products for babies and toddlers. There's a great collection of charming clothes made from organic cotton and wool, and toys from untreated wood. Best of all, everything is absolutely delightful without being overly cute.

Frederiksberg Allé 70, 1820 Frederiksberg C
www.aniel.dk

7 Karmaman

Karmaman food market is an exciting combination of a café, restaurant, wine bar and deli. Colourful art on the walls and in the windows bring a friendly atmosphere to this large space. At lunchtime this is a favourite spot for local office workers, who come for the freshly prepared food, and from the late afternoon onwards, people drop in for a glass of wine. But this is also a perfect spot if you just want a cup of coffee and a break.

Frederiksberg Allé 31, 1851 Frederiksberg
www.karmaman.dk

Stephanie, Bredgade

8 Designdelicatessen

This is a general store full of good design. The Designdelicatessen is a large online store that sells everything that makes homes more beautiful, from furniture to light bulbs. The brick-and-mortar shop in Frederiksberg serves as a showroom for only a fraction of Designdelicatessen's enormous range, even though it extends over several levels. Buy a Copenhagen poster as a perfect souvenir—the staff will be happy to pack it safely inside a tube for your journey home.

Frederiksberg Allé 6, 1820 Frederiksberg
www.designdelicatessen.com

9 Granola

The Værnedamsvej is the border between Frederiksberg and Vesterbro, so crossing the road also means stepping into another suburb. But that doesn't make much difference for people strolling along this street, and everybody eventually meets at Granola anyway. This is a wonderfully nostalgic café with an old counter from colonial times. The smoothies are fabulous, as are the waffles, which are also sold through a side window.

Værnedamsvej 5, 1819 Frederiksberg
www.granola.dk

10 Blomsterskuret

Blomsterskuret is directly next door to Granola. The name translates as 'flower shed', which is a very apt description. The baskets and buckets outside the store are full of luscious greenery year round; you may find plants growing from old filing boxes and on Europallets, and ferns suspended from the somewhat sagging awning. It's all a bit chaotic, but incredibly charming, and it adds a lovely touch of green and fun to your stroll along this busy street.

Værnedamsvej 3A, 1819 Frederiksberg C
www.blomsterskuret.dk

11 Rist Kaffebar

Rist Kaffebar is tiny. There are only a few tables inside, next to the counter, and a few more outside. But the coffee here is truly outstanding, which is why you'll often find a queue, sometimes even stretching outside along the street. If you are lucky enough to score one of the tables, then sit down and enjoy the wonderful atmosphere while you nibble on cookies, sip your hot drink and just people-watch.

Værnedamsvej 4B, 1619 København V
www.ristkaffebar.dk

Wide, tree-lined streets are typical of Frederiksberg.

12 Jérôme Vintage

The fashion boutique Jérôme Vintage opened only quite recently, somewhat hidden in a side street basement, but is definitely worth going out of your way to find. You may not even notice that every item of exquisite women's fashion sold here is second-hand. Admire individual pieces by Bottega Veneta, Céline and Saint Laurent, among others, displayed on racks sorted by colour, like textile works of art. A small selection of shoes perfectly complements the already outstanding range.

Tullinsgade 12, 1618 København V

13 Can

Can is like a bag of mixed sweets: colourful, cheerful and a little crazy. The store is run by friends Stine, Pac and Sofia, and each of the owners makes an idiosyncratic contribution to the objects on offer. Pac sells old vinyl records, Stine exhibits her illustrations and Sofia makes toys by hand. Sometimes you can even get a haircut in the rear of the shop, and on weekends there are often exhibitions, concerts and parties.

Tullinsgade 5, 1618 København V
www.yeswecancan.com

14 Falernum

This wine bar is the perfect place to unwind after a long day. The atmosphere is cosy, with small, candle-lit tables, the clientele is very relaxed and the tapas are even more delicious with a glass of lovely wine—the friendly staff will be happy to help you make a selection. Falernum is also open throughout the day, when you can sit outside in the sun. The kitchen does breakfast, salads and sandwiches.

Værnedamsvej 16, 1619 København V
www.falernum.dk

15 Juul's Vin og Spiritus

If a visit to Falernum has inspired you about good wine, make sure to drop in at Juul's wine store directly opposite. Juul's stocks an incredible range of wines and spirits, especially whiskeys. The knowledgeable staff give competent advice without the slightest hint of superiority, even to absolute novices. If you ask nicely, you may even be able to taste, but the store also offers tasting sessions quite regularly.

Værnedamsvej 15, 1819 Frederiksberg
www.juuls.dk

16 Black

Danish ceramic artist Anne Black has been selling ceramics from her studio next door for some time, but it is her menswear store on Gammel Kongevej that attracts visitors from all over the city. Raw concrete walls form the backdrop for high-quality basics by renowned labels including Margaret Howell and Comme des Garçons. There is also a fine selection of home accessories and art magazines. Black is yet another store that does stylish minimalism to perfection.

Gammel Kongevej 105, 1850 Frederiksberg
www.blackcph.com

17 Sound Station

Copenhagen has its fair share of vinyl fans, and Sound Station is their heaven on earth. The store stocks an incredible 200,000 LPs and CDs, from obscure Danish pop songs through to old-school hip-hop from the 1980s. The walls are decorated with rare Gold records donated to Sound Station by various musicians during their visits to this Copenhagen institution.

Gammel Kongevej 94, 1850 Frederiksberg
www.soundstation.dk

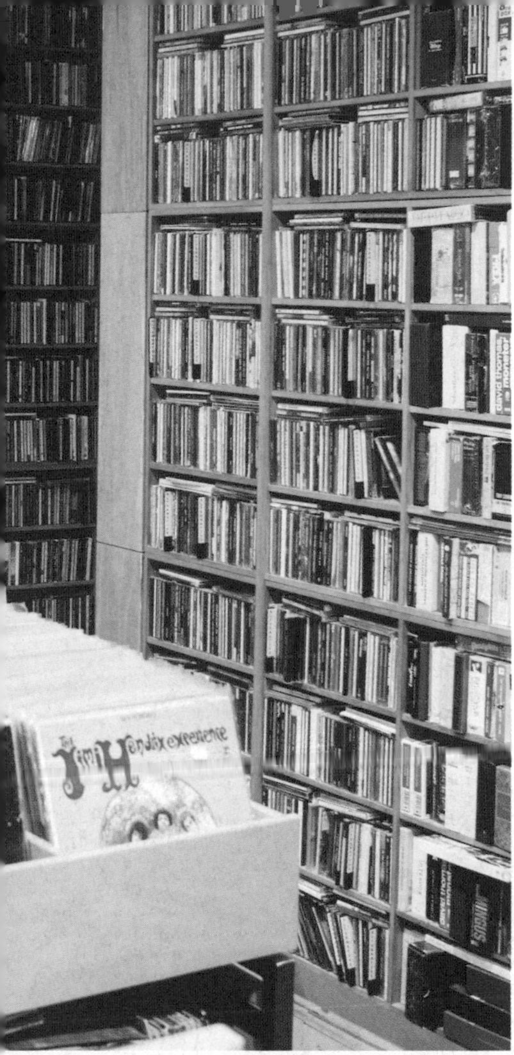

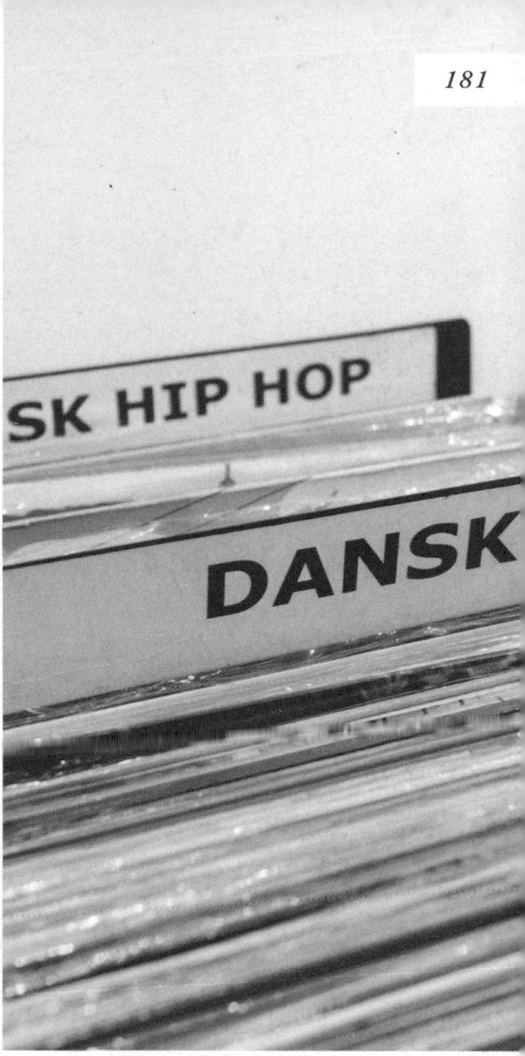
SK HIP HOP
DANSK

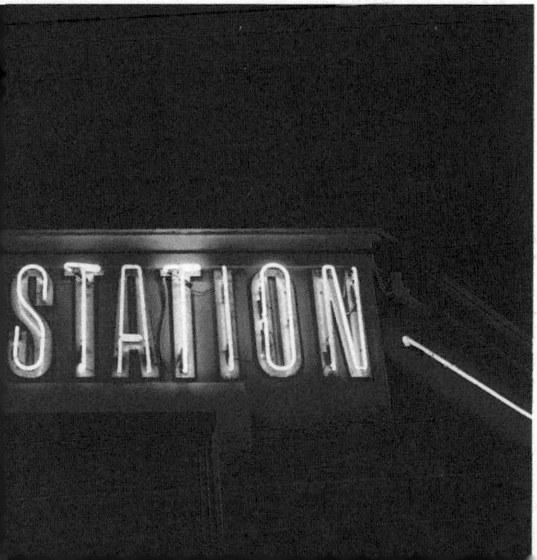
STATION

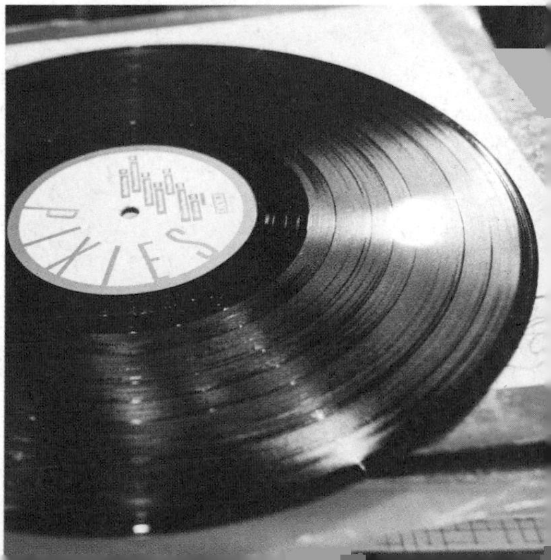
PIXIES

18 Frederiksberg Mansion B&B

This romantic bed and breakfast is in a quiet residential street in the heart of Frederiksberg, but by public transport it only takes a few minutes to get to the city centre. The stylish, historic mansion has six guest rooms, all of them individually furnished and decorated, most with private bathrooms. A delicious breakfast and Wi-Fi are included, and the roof terrace is a great feature in summer.

Jacobys Allé 21, 1806 Frederiksberg C
www.frederiksbergmansion.dk

19 Frederiksberg
Flea Market

One of Copenhagen's most popular flea markets is held outside Frederiksberg Town Hall from 9 am to 3 pm every Saturday between April and October. Locals from Frederiksberg and the surrounding suburbs sell their treasures here, often including quite a few high fashion brands and, of course, furniture. Come early for the best finds. There are beer stalls and live music, too.

Allégade, 2000 Frederiksberg

PETER N.
DUPONT

The Coffee Collective coffee roasters are renowned for their excellent coffee well beyond Denmark. They operate three cafés in Copenhagen and sell their roasted beans all over the world. Managing Director Peter N. Dupont explains why the company's active social engagement for the rights of its coffee farmers is a good thing for everybody, and tells us about his favourite restaurants.

What is the Coffee Collective?
We are four partners, who founded the Coffee Collective in 2007. At the time we all worked for another coffee company, but we had the feeling that we would be able to build up an enterprise that could take quality, and more importantly its trade with producers, a step further. Klaus Thomsen, one of our partners, was the world champion barista at the time, and I sourced and roasted the coffee he used for the competition, so we were quite sure that we would be able to deliver quality that people would appreciate. Our goal was to implement a business model that was all about quality. We wanted to bring to consumers the level of quality we had experienced at competitions. At the time, the market for high-quality coffee was growing rapidly, and I believe it hasn't stopped expanding since.
This level of quality would come at a price?
Yes, and customers are very much ready to pay a higher price for higher quality. Our coffee is more expensive than that of other roasters because we want to pay local producers higher, fair prices, and our customers are very much on our side. This gives coffee farmers an opportunity and

incentive to produce ever better beans. For us it means an even better end product that allows us to maintain our position as truly superior coffee roasters. It's a positive circle that underpins everything the Coffee Collective does. The four of us all believe very strongly in this idea, which has drawn us together, despite our very different backgrounds.
What are your various backgrounds?
I have a Master of Science in International Development Studies, Klaus Thomsen is an award-winning barista with many years of experience, Linus Törsäter graduated in architecture, and Casper Rasmussen, our fourth man, has a background in catering and business. He also won the 2008 coffee tasting world championship in Denmark, just a year after we established the Coffee Collective. His win so soon after we had opened really gave us a huge boost. The title is a real accolade among coffee fans and gave us a lot of publicity in the coffee scene.
The coffee scene seems to be a fairly tight-knit community in which word about world championship titles spreads really quickly. Would that be right?
Definitely! But the internet and social media are also really helpful. For die-hard fans, baristas are almost like rock stars, at least in the Western world. And producers like me build up networks across the whole planet, so we can truly speak of a worldwide community with quality and sustainability at its heart. That's one of the most exciting aspects of my job, I find.
The Coffee Collective is also very influential at the local level—there are people who visit Copenhagen just because of you! Being a local company, do you feel like you're part of the city?

I'm really happy to hear that! I was born in Copenhagen and have lived here for most of my life, so I feel a very close connection with the city, and that's the same for all four of us. We also try to express this connection through various little gestures. For example, our internet address has always been *coffeecollective.dk* and not .com, because we wanted to make a point of being located in Denmark. The .com address was available at the time, but we didn't want it. Someone else has taken it in the meantime and sometimes pretends to be us.

Let's talk a little about the city.
Which are your favourite restaurants?

People in Copenhagen are incredibly spoiled because there are so many good restaurants. I have three absolute favourites: *Relæ* (p. 134) is the most creative and experimental of all of them, as far as I'm concerned. I love cuisine that explores the limits of what is possible, even if it means that it sometimes goes beyond these limits. A meal at this restaurant can touch you more deeply than you may initially think. It touches you on an emotional level, and that's just fantastic. I also love the elegance, aromas and flavours of *Kiin Kiin*, and my third favourite is *Kadeau* (p. 120), which I think truly embodies the Danish approach to design: an atmosphere, a team and cuisine that represent Bornholm through and through and achieve amazing feats.

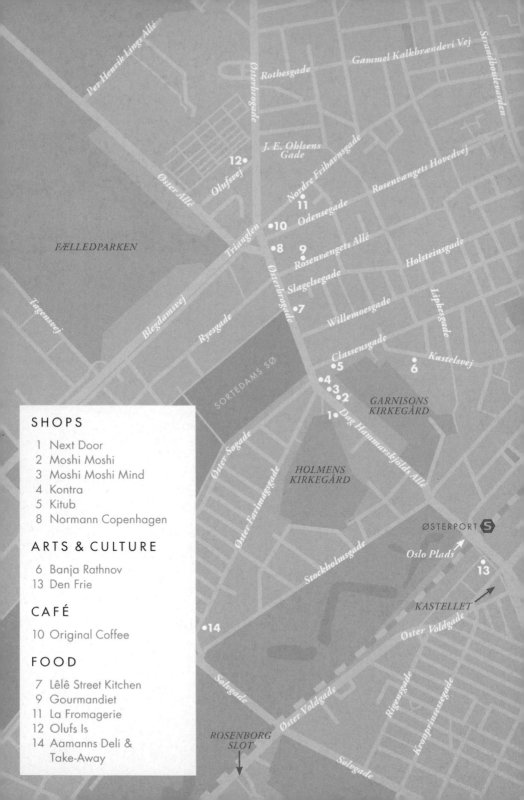

SHOPS

1 Next Door
2 Moshi Moshi
3 Moshi Moshi Mind
4 Kontra
5 Kitub
8 Normann Copenhagen

ARTS & CULTURE

6 Banja Rathnov
13 Den Frie

CAFÉ

10 Original Coffee

FOOD

7 Lêlê Street Kitchen
9 Gourmandiet
11 La Fromagerie
12 Olufs Is
14 Aamanns Deli &
   Take-Away

ØSTERBRO

Idyllic, lush Østerbro is one of Copenhagen's most attractive residential areas, and a lot of families with children live in this suburb in Copenhagen's north. But Østerbro is also worth a visit for tourists: there's Fælledparken, Denmark's largest park, and the world-famous bronze statue of the Little Mermaid. The suburb offers great shopping, at a much more leisurely pace than in the inner city. Finally, there are many small restaurants vying to be discovered as the next insider tip.

1 Next Door

'Recycle your rooms' is the motto of the mother-daughter team running Next Door. While their main purpose is to give a new life to antiques and second-hand furniture, they also provide a fair amount of inspiration for your own home. Next Door is refreshingly different: with plenty of wood, gold, brass and wallpaper featuring tropical motifs, this store embodies opulence much more than cool Scandinavian restraint.

Dag Hammarskjölds Allé 33,
2100 København Ø

2 Moshi Moshi

The Moshi Moshi family comprises three stores, two of them immediately next to each other. Moshi Moshi, one of Copenhagen's most beautifully designed women's fashion boutiques, stocks a small, yet exquisite selection of clothes in toned-down colours from labels including Isabel Marant and Frame Jeans. Next door, Moshi Moshi Shoes is all about great bags, a lovely selection of jewellery and, of course, shoes.

Dag Hammarskjölds Allé 34,
2100 København Ø
www.moshimoshi.dk

3 Moshi Moshi Mind

While the other two stores in the Moshi Moshi family focus on the worldly side of life, Moshi Moshi Mind caters to more spiritual aspirations, with a large range of comfortable yoga clothes and sportswear, teas, organic cosmetics, comfortable loungewear and posters with motivational quotes. However, Moshi Moshi Mind is not at all an esoteric, out-of-this-world universe; the store is inviting, clear and bright, with very helpful staff.

Dag Hammarskjölds Allé 40, 2100
København Ø | www.moshimoshimind.dk

4 Kontra

Kontra sells everything you need to make great coffee at home, starting with high-quality espresso machines, which are lined up at the rear of the store, through to filters, various coffee-making utensils and, of course, the very best coffee beans. The beans are probably Kontra's main attraction for tourists: Troels Poulsen, one of the store owners, won the barista world championships in 2005.

Dag Hammarskjölds Allé 36,
2100 København Ø
www.kontracoffee.com

5 Kitub

Cleaning is not the most exciting of
activities, and it's not likely that any
cleaning utensil will ever change that,
but Kitub does everything it can to raise
the aesthetics of everyday cleaning. This
tiny store stocks handmade dusters, brushes
with natural bristles, beautiful table linen
and even stylish cleaning cloths, plus
a lot of useful textiles such as towels,
gloves and scarves, and a regularly
changing selection of ceramics.

Classensgade 10, 2100 København Ø
www.kitub.com

6 Banja Rathnov

This is a lovely, expansive art gallery in a historical building. While Banja Rathnov's exhibition space is somewhat hidden in the courtyard of a residential building, it features exciting, frequently award-winning exhibitions of Danish and international artists. The building is large enough to have at least two shows on at any given time. The programme changes regularly and admission is free.

Kastelsvej 18, 2100 København Ø
www.banjarathnov.com

7 Lêlê Street Kitchen

The original Lêlê in Vesterbro serves Asian cuisine with flavours and prices that are at Michelin star levels, but luckily for us there's an inexpensive offshoot, Lêlê Street Kitchen, with much lower prices. The menu features healthy, homemade Vietnamese fast food: spring rolls, salads and soups, served with plenty of vegetables and fresh herbs. Dine in or order take-away.

Østerbrogade 56, 2100 København Ø
www.lele.dk

Lasse, Julius Thomsens Plads

8 Normann Copenhagen

This label, founded by two locals only in 1999, quickly established itself as one of the most successful and best known Danish design houses and currently exports to over seventy-seven countries. Its 1700-square-metre flagship store in a former cinema directly on Østerbro's main boulevard stocks Normann Copenhagen's full product range. From large pieces of furniture to exquisite flower arrangements, these are displayed in themes around the store.

Østerbrogade 70, 2100 København Ø
www.normann-copenhagen.com

9 *Gourmandiet*

Gourmandiet is quite rightly considered Copenhagen's most beautiful butcher's shop. It was recently lovingly restored to its former glory, including the nineteenth-century murals and ceiling paintings. Gourmandiet sells Danish specialties (including vegetarian ones!) and lunches. Every Thursday, Friday and Saturday night, this simple butcher's shop becomes the first-class steakhouse Gourmandiet by Night.

Rosenvængets Allé 7A, 2100 København Ø
www.gourmandiet.dk

KAFFE		KOLDE DRIKKE	
DRIP COFFEE	30;	SMOOTHIES	37;
ESPRESSO	20/25;	ISKAFFE	37;
ESPRESSO M.	22/27;	ANTONS JUICE	22;
AMERICANO	30;		
CORTADO	32;		
EN FOSS	35;	DET SØDE	
CAFÉ LATTE	32/37;	CROISSANT	15;

10 Original Coffee

Original Coffee has four cafés in Copenhagen, and its small Østerbro branch has repeatedly won awards as the city's best coffee shop. The building also houses the micro-roastery where beans for the cafés are produced. This tiny place is always busy: the homemade cookies alone are worth a visit, but if you like something stronger, Original Coffee's Irish Coffee is absolutely exquisite. You can even get a beer here.

Nordre Frihavnsgade 4, 2100 København Ø
www.originalcoffee.dk

In Denmark, prams are parked outside—with the babies.

11 La Fromagerie

This is a little piece of France right in the heart of Østerbro. La Fromagerie is run by a very charming Frenchman, who shares his wealth of knowledge about his produce in a delightful French accent. La Fromagerie stocks not only cheese, but also some specialty sausages and jams, plus little delicacies from Denmark and the rest of Europe. While the focus is on French cheese, there are also some delectable Danish cheeses that are well worth tasting.

Nordre Frihavnsgade 16, 2100 København Ø
www.lafromagerie.dk

12 Olufs Is

Copenhagen's best ice cream is found at Olufs Is. But don't expect tubs, cups or waffles; instead you'll find a huge range of homemade popsicles: ice creams and sorbets, often dipped in chocolate and decorated with berries, praline or cookie crumbles. Olufs Is is closed in winter, but its season is still long: most years, the shop is open between March and November— just check the website.

Olufsvej 6, 2100 København Ø
www.olufs.dk

13 Den Frie

Den Frie Centre of Contemporary Art has established itself as a modern art institution. Founded by a group of modern artists as early as 1898, this museum has become one of the mainstays of the Copenhagen arts scene. The centre exhibits new, exciting art by up-and-coming artists under its motto 'By artists—for everyone'. It often focuses on exhibitions by artist collectives and other creative groups.

Oslo Plads 1, 2100 København Ø
www.denfrie.dk

14 Aamanns Deli & Take-Away

Smørrebrød is as Danish as it gets, and in Copenhagen smørrebrød doesn't get better than at Aamanns. Adam Aamanns' modern interpretations of these traditional rye sandwiches are small works of art, generously topped with smoked fish, roast beef, egg or even potato. Eat inside or get a selection to take away for a typically Danish picnic in the park.

Øster Farimagsgade 10, 2100 København Ø
www.aamanns.dk

KASPER
HOSTRUP

It isn't just Danish women who dress well, Copenhagen men also seem to have an excellent sense of what looks good. Kasper Hostrup, owner of the popular Østerbro menswear boutique Goods, shares his thoughts about male style and good design and lets us in on his favourite spots in this suburb.

What is it that makes Goods different?
We try to stock a selection of high-quality products that all follow our idiosyncratic line, so the Goods strategy is in fact very simple: good quality and good design.

Who shops at Goods?
We attract a very broad clientele. Actually you can find all age groups in our store, at least anybody between twenty-five and seventy-five, because we aren't quite out there enough for the really young age group. This age range is also reflected in what we stock: our clothes are simple, without a lot of adornment, but always sophisticated and contemporary. A few years ago, the trend towards heritage fashion started, that is fashion oriented quite strongly along classical designs, usually American, such as leather boots, lumberjack shirts and dark, non-faded denim. We sell this stuff, but always try to find more contemporary and relevant interpretations.

Why did you choose to open your store in Østerbro?
I looked at stores in Frederiksberg and Østerbro, but ultimately it simply made more sense to go to Østerbro, as there was no other place similar to ours. The store has since developed into a business that is quite unique in Copenhagen. Other men's fashion stores that we compete with, for example Norse Projects and Wood Wood, come from a skateboarding and graffiti background, whereas our approach to menswear is more mature and modern.

How would you describe the style of Copenhagen men?
It's tricky to put into just a few words. There are many different styles, but I think in the past five years there has been a clear trend towards men becoming very conscious of the quality of their clothes. Durability is a lot more important now than it was ten years ago. Male shoppers are now prepared to pay more for an individual item than they were then.

Do you have any tips for men visiting Copenhagen, if they haven't found their own, personal style yet?
First things first: there's nothing that's an absolute no-no in fashion. Fashion should enhance your personality and character and show off your best side. So if you want to stroll through Copenhagen in white socks and sandals—go for it, nobody will stop you. Copenhagen is very tolerant as far as personal style is concerned.

Yet there is something like a 'Danish uniform', which you see more commonly here than elsewhere.
That's true. Start with the cut. Many men make the mistake of buying clothes that don't really sit well on them. Either their pants and jackets are much too big, or they wear T-shirts that are two sizes too small. Make sure you get a well-cut item, and you're halfway there. The next consideration is quality. It's better to invest in one piece that you'll still wear in five years' time than in five short-lived designs from a cheaper store. By doing that, you'll gradually build up a wardrobe that is not only high in quality, but also

features great, timeless, contemporary design. After all, nobody wants to keep wearing T-shirts with the same funny slogans for five years.

*What are your favourite spots
in the neighbourhood?*

Østerbro sometimes feels like a small town, and I know many of the shop, restaurant, bar and café owners personally—that's what makes it so interesting for me to be here. A totally amazing furniture store recently opened across the street from us, called *Next Door* (p. 190). There's also *Gourmandiet* (p. 202) on Rosenvængets Allé, an old butcher's shop that has been there for about a hundred years. It was some other type of shop at some stage, but then it was taken over by a butcher again, who restored the old murals with a lot of love and care. It's the most beautiful butcher's shop I've ever seen! And the entire area around Bopa Plads is really charming.

*Do you have some favourite
restaurants you can recommend?*

I very much like *Davids Bistro* on Åhusgade, a really lovely place. I usually recommend *Aamanns* (p. 209) to all of my customers and tell them to try the smørrebrød there. Østerbro has a lot of small places that are easily overlooked if you don't know what you're looking for, including *Original Coffee* (p. 203), where I go almost every morning to have coffee and read the paper.

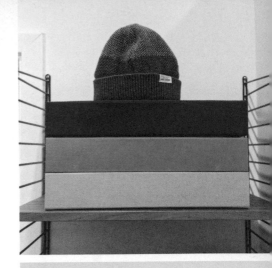

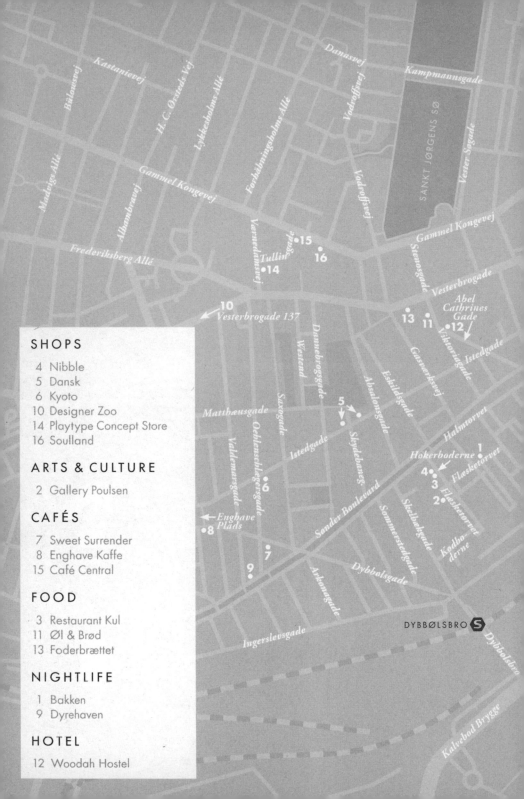

VESTERBRO

N

Welcome to Vesterbro! Until fairly recently, few Copenhageners would have ventured into this area around the city's central station, a quarter dominated by red-light establishments, factories and the wholesale food market. But Vesterbro has undergone a transformation that has seen it become the city's coolest area. Some streets may still feel a bit seedy, but all around them are Copenhagen's most exciting clubs and bars, trendy fashion boutiques, art galleries and inviting parks full of street art.

1 Bakken

Copenhagen's nightlife pulsates in the Meatpacking District, which was once home to the city's main wholesale food market. The city's chefs still come here to buy fresh produce, including meat, but many of the old market halls are no longer in use except as cheap venues for clubs, bars and start-ups. Among these is Bakken, one of Copenhagen's best clubs. To find your way around, just follow the colourful fairy lights ...

Flæsketorvet 19–21, 1712 København V
www.bakkenkbh.dk

'From New York!
Garde Now
'09 – 08/11

2 Gallery Poulsen

One of the city's most popular art galleries can also be found in the Meatpacking District: Gallery Poulsen represents mainly American artists, and includes some superstars, such as Leonard Cohen and Danish supermodel Helena Christensen, who is also a successful photographer. The gallery's focus is on figurative art, painting, graffiti and photography, much of which is quite colourful. Admission is free.

Flæsketorvet 24, 1711 København V
www.gallerypoulsen.com

3 Restaurant Kul

This is a barbecue restaurant that has shed every last bit of the old steakhouse concept. All dishes served at Restaurant Kul are prepared either directly on the barbecue or in a barbecue oven. Smoky aromas waft through the dining area; the atmosphere is relaxed, and the waiters encourage guests to order a number of smaller dishes to share. While the food served is of a very high standard, the prices are moderate. On weekends it's best to book ahead.

Høkerboderne 16B–20, 1712 København V
www.restaurantkul.dk

4 Nibble

Nibble is a paradise for foodies and bookworms. It is operated by the I'm Kombo collective of chefs and gastronomical innovators, who have embarked on a mission to stock all major contemporary food and cooking magazines on the market. Nibble also has a selection of design objects and special edition products associated with food and drink, from limited-edition beers to sneakers featuring bacon print.

Høkerboderne 16, 1712 København V
www.nibbleshop.com

Start your visit to Vesterbro at Vesterport station.

VESTERBRO

5 Dansk

The Dansk label comprises two interiors shops located only a few steps apart. Dansk Made for Rooms was established first and sells furniture and interior decorations. DanskKitchen, a few doors further along the street, is all about clever kitchen accessories from all over the world. The owners frequently travel to Asia and America to source the best pots, pans and utensils for today's sophisticated kitchen.

Istedgade 64 & 80, 1650 København V
www.danskmadeforrooms.dk

6 Kyoto

Kyoto, Vesterbro's most popular fashion store, started out selling only menswear but, to the delight of its fans, expanded its range and now sells both men's and women's fashion. This store on Istedgade stocks many major Scandinavian labels, such as Libertine-Libertine, Diana Orving and Wood Wood, next to a lovely selection of other international designers, including Kitsuné and Pendleton. The Kyoto range also features shoes, jewellery and underwear.

Istedgade 95, 1650 København V
www.kyoto.dk

7 Sweet Surrender

Copenhagen is very child friendly, and so it comes as no surprise that there are more and more children's cafés opening. Sweet Surrender was one of the first that specifically catered to the needs of parents and their children. There's a generous play area, a breastfeeding space and a child-friendly menu with unsweetened juices, teas and yummy baked goods. You don't have children? Not to worry, you can lean back on one of the comfy sofas all by yourself.

Dybbølsgade 49, 1721 København V
www.sweetsurrender.dk

8 Enghave Kaffe

Enghave Kaffe looks like a bikies' bar: there are motorbike drawings on the counter and helmets hung along the walls, the lighting is dim and the guys behind the counter are tattooed and on the heavy side. But Enghave serves coffee, not hard liquor, and there's cheerful rockabilly playing in the background. The specialty coffees are excellent, and it's all very comfortable, but make sure you leave your laptop stashed away—it's a strictly computer-free zone!

Enghave Plads 3, 1670 København V
www.enghavekaffe.dk

Line, Pilestræde

9 Dyrehaven

This place, once a dark and dingy bar, has become a firm favourite with Copenhagen's hipsters. It has retained the old wooden counter and quirky hunting trophies on the wall and serves traditional Danish food. Dyrehaven is a very popular restaurant in the evenings, so it's best to come early to get a table. On weekends, the kitchen closes at 9 pm and Dyrehaven morphs into one of the city's best bars.

Sønder Boulevard 72, 1720 København V
www.dyrehavnkbh.dk

Monsieur

10 Designer Zoo

This large, two-storey building is an outlet for more than seventy Danish artisans and designers. The main focus is on ceramics, glass, jewellery and fabric design, but you'll also find handmade furniture and fashion accessories. You can even visit the seven studios at the rear and watch the artists at work. Designer Zoo also organises regularly changing exhibitions. *Vesterbrogade 137, 1620 København V*
www.dzoo.dk

11 Øl & Brød

When the restaurant next to the first branch of Mikkeller brewery became vacant, the Mikkeller team grabbed the opportunity and opened its first restaurant, Øl & Brød. The name is also a mission statement: the place serves beer and bread, nothing else, except Akvavit spirits. Don't worry: its two young chefs use fresh Danish ingredients to make excellent smørrebrøds. And the beer obviously comes from Mikkeller.

Viktoriagade 6, 1655 København V
www.ologbrod.dk

12 Woodah Hostel

Just supplying linen is so yesterday!
The Woodah Hostel service goes that little
bit further (although linen is also provided)
and offers its guests an hour of yoga every
day in its own yoga studio. What better
way to start the day before exploring the
city? Woodah has two dormitories and
a double room at inexpensive, hostel prices.
Vegetarian breakfast is included in the rate.
Abel Cathrines Gade 1–3, 1654 København V
www.woodah-hostel.com

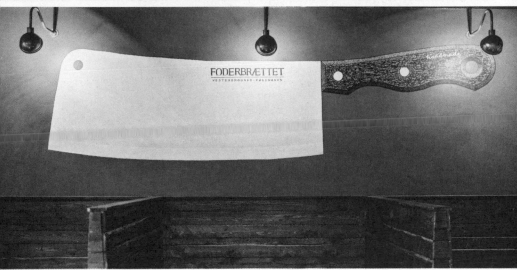

13 Foderbrættet

Foderbrættet, loosely translated as 'Feeding Place', is Copenhagen's first hot-dog restaurant. The menu features hot dogs in all imaginable and exotic variations, served with proper champagne and rather excellent cocktails. Factor in at least two hot dogs if you're hungry! On weekend nights, when the restaurant has DJs spinning music, it develops a happening bar vibe and can get pretty busy.

Vesterbrogade 41, 1620 København V
www.foderbraettetkbh.dk

Virgil, Ny Vestergade

14 Playtype Concept Store

Playtype is a renowned agency that develops fonts and sells its designs to customers across the globe. Its concept store is the first brick-and-mortar store for fonts and font-related merchandise. Sit at a computer with one of the designers to develop your own font and take the file straight home. The store sells everything you can put a letter on: posters, clothes, mugs, laptop sleeves and skateboards.

Værnedamsvej 6, 1620 København V
www.playtype.com

15 Café Central

If you believe the owners of Copenhagen's Café Central, this tiny place is the proud holder of two records: with only five seats it's the city's smallest café, and with only one room it's the world's smallest hotel. The café sources its beans from Coffee Collective and serves sandwiches, banana splits and traditional sweets from the 1980s (notably Hubba Bubba and Spunk candy). The cute double room is upstairs.

Tullinsgade 1, 1618 København V
www.centralhotelogcafe.dk

16 Soulland

Soulland was opened by Silas Adler in 2002 and has established itself as one of Denmark's major men's fashion labels for streetwear. Its flagship store in Vesterbro stocks the full current collection as well as limited editions from partnerships that Soulland regularly organises with other brands. The shirts and jumpers designed by Soulland in collaboration with the illustrators of Babar the Elephant are legendary.

Gammel Kongevej 37, 1610 København V
www.soulland.com

BUTCHERS & BICYCLES

MORTEN WAGENER
JAKOB MUNK
MORTEN MOGENSEN

Bicycles are Copenhageners' favourite means of transport. You'll also see cargo bikes on the streets, which fit, young parents often use to ferry their kids and shopping around. Butchers & Bicycles is a start-up enterprise that has taken up a mission to build the world's best cargo bikes. We have interviewed its founders about their love of cargo bikes and Copenhagen's bicycle culture.

Your company is still young— how long has it been around?

Jakob Munk: We started in November 2013, but the two Mortens worked on our prototype long before we opened. They spent three-and-a-half years perfecting its design, and when we finally launched it on the market, it took off like a rocket.

How did you come up with your ~~unusual~~ company name?

J.M.: We called ourselves Butchers & Bicycles because our workshop and office space is in Copenhagen's Meatpacking District. We were looking to express our connection to this area.

Your showroom looks great. What's the story behind it?

J.M.: The premises used to be a falafel factory. We spent weeks scrubbing falafel oil from the walls, and had 17 tons of concrete poured on the floor. The tiled walls were kept as a homage to the old butcher's shop, though. This is our showroom, office and assembly workshop. We source our parts from all over the world, store them here and then assemble the bikes by hand as the orders come in.

What's so special about your bikes?

Morten Wagener: We just love cycling! Cargo bikes are nothing new in Copenhagen, and people are used to taking their kids and lots of stuff on their bikes all over the city. The traditional three-wheeled cargo bikes were very heavy and difficult to maneouvre, but they were still very popular because they are just so incredibly useful. We are great fans of this mode of transport, but we always thought that the old models left a lot of room for improvement. It was a real challenge to ride them fast or over extended periods.

What is it that you do differently in your bikes?

M.W.: We wanted to combine all of the advantages of these great, three-wheeled cargo bikes with the fabulous feeling you get when you cycle through the city on a normal bike. Our bikes lean into curves, and once you have got used to them— which doesn't take long—they feel just like a standard bike. You get around very quickly, you're not a nuisance to other traffic, and for kids sitting in the cargo area in front it's almost as exciting as a rollercoaster ride. All of our designs, all of the decisions we take when building these bikes, go back to wanting to create the very best riding experience. If our customers enjoy riding their bikes, they'll use them more often, it's that simple. But we've also added a lot of small details that really make a difference: the cargo area has a child lock, safety belts and a door for quick entry and exit. You can get a rainproof version, and you can even fit child seats!

Who are your customers?

M.W.: There are about 40,000 cargo bikes in Copenhagen alone, so the Danish market is quite large, even for a niche product such as ours. Our customers are mainly families with one or two children.

One in four families in Copenhagen has a cargo bike; they are incredibly popular. Without them, inner city traffic would be gridlocked. Our customers actually buy these bikes instead of a car. Other countries also look at our city and its bicycle culture as a model that they may want to follow.

Why is it that the Danes love bicycles so much?

J.M.: The main reason is that it's practical. Bicycles are part of our everyday lives; they are simply the fastest way of getting around. Copenhagen also has an incredible cycling infrastructure, with bicycle freeways and foot rests for cyclists at traffic lights, so that cyclists don't have to dismount when they wait. We even have rubbish bins installed at an angle next to bike paths so you can throw your rubbish in while cycling past.

What are your favourite spots in Copenhagen?

M.W.: I love going to *Lidkoeb*, a bar on Vesterbrogade, before going out to dinner. It's a former pharmacy, a beautiful space with a log fire, and the bar staff have a real passion for mixing cocktails.

J.M.: My personal favourite is the restaurant *Höst* (p. 88). That's where I send everybody who asks me where to find good, inexpensive Scandinavian food.

Your favourite cycling route?

M.W.: Anything that's along the water. I love cycling along the shore on weekends and sitting down with a beer after a long tour, just looking out at the sea.

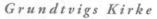

Grundtvigs Kirke

Although Grundtvigs Kirke is a simple, unadorned church, it is breathtakingly beautiful. The space is bright and flooded with natural light, and the Gothic Revival façade on the western side could be straight out of a fantasy movie. The church was built in honour of the Danish philosopher and pastor Nikolai Frederik Severin Grundtvig. It holds 1800 people, making it Denmark's largest church by capacity. It was constructed using six million pale yellow bricks.

På Bjerget 14b, 2400 København NV
www.grundtvigskirke.dk

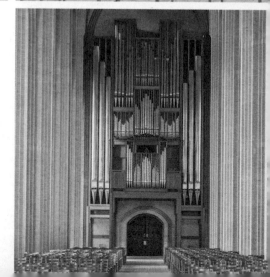

COPENHAGEN

Amager Beach

When Copenhageners want to relax, they go to Amager Beach, a very picturesque stretch of coast that was widened with sand excavated during the construction of the famous Øresund Bridge. Amager Beach is all about relaxing and exercising outdoors: enjoy the lagoon in the centre of the area or work out in the kayaking facilities and 1000-metre swimming lanes. There are public showers and a lovely view across to Sweden on the other side of the bridge.

Amager Strandvej 110, 2300 København S
www.amager-strand.dk

Humlebæk●

Copenhagen

HOVEDSTADEN

Louisiana

The Louisiana Museum of Modern Art, 40 kilometres north of the city, is definitely worth a little detour. The museum, Denmark's major centre of modern and contemporary art, attracts the world's best artists, who regularly hold excellent exhibitions here. The building is beautifully located in a rugged, typically Danish landscape; many of its spaces, including the sculpture garden, have great views of the sea.

Gammel Strandvej 13, 3050 Humlebæk
www.louisiana.dk

INDEX

AUTHOR

Anna Peuckert

Anna Peuckert comes from Cologne; she's a journalist who mainly writes on fashion, lifestyle and travel. In 2013 she established the website 12hrs.net together with Søren Jepsen to invite readers on short city trips off the beaten tourist tracks. Anna's travel stories explore good design, fashion and food.

PHOTOGRAPHER

Søren Jepsen

Søren Jepsen is a photographer and blogger from Copenhagen. For the past eight years Søren has been portraying the stylishly dressed people he has encountered in cities around the world in his street style blog, thelocals.dk. He also regularly does photo shoots for magazines and websites. Visit his travel blog, 12hrs.net, for photos from his travels.

First published by National Geographic Germany in 2015
Updated and published in 2016 by Murdoch Books, an imprint of Allen & Unwin

Murdoch Books Australia
83 Alexander Street
Crows Nest NSW 2065
Phone: +61 (0) 2 8425 0100
www.murdochbooks.com.au
info@murdochbooks.com.au

Murdoch Books UK
Erico House, 6th Floor
93-99 Upper Richmond Road
Putney, London SW15 2TG
Phone: +44 (0) 20 8785 5995
www.murdochbooks.co.uk
info@murdochbooks.co.uk

For Corporate Orders & Custom Publishing contact Noel Hammond,
National Business Development Manager, Murdoch Books Australia

Publisher: Corinne Roberts
Photos: Søren Jepsen
Text: Anna Peuckert
Idea: Stephanie Jaeschke, Søren Jepsen, Anna Peuckert
Lithography: Peter Becker GmbH, Würzburg
Design and cartography: Tina Strube | books and infographics

Translator: Claudia McQuillan
Editorial Manager: Jane Price
Editor: Shan Wolody
Design Manager: Madeleine Kane
Cover Design: Susanne Geppert
Production Manager: Mary Bjelobrk

Copyright © NG-Malik Buch GmbH

A cataloguing-in-publication entry is available from the catalogue
of the National Library of Australia at nla.gov.au.
ISBN 978 1 76029 090 0 Australia
ISBN 978 1 74336 732 2 UK
A catalogue record for this book is available from the British Library.

Colour reproduction by Splitting Image, Clayton, Victoria
Printed by 1010 Printing International Limited, China

ADDITIONAL PHOTO CREDITS
Front cover: centre far right © Alastair Philip Wiper, bottom far left © Kristian Ridder-Nielsen; Pages 34–35: top left, top right and bottom right © Designmuseum Danmark, bottom left and centre right © Pernille Klemp; Page 36: © Stamers Kontor; Pages 56–57: bottom © Inez Dawczyk; Page 73: top © Royal Copenhagen; Page 85: bottom left © Stamers Kontor; Page 92: top © Ole Haupt, bottom © Kim Nilsson; Pages 104–105: top left, right and bottom right © Kristian Ridder-Nielsen; Page 106: centre left © Culinaire Saisonnier; Pages 110–111: © Alastair Philip Wiper; Page 117: © Anders Sune Berg; Page 118: bottom left © Henrik Krarup Smith; Pages 120–123: © Marie Louise Munkegaard; Page 183: top left © Christian Alsing, bottom left © Cees van Roeden; Page 207: © Thomas Adotcom; Page 209: top and centre right © Mikkel Hvilshøj, bottom left © Columbus Leth; Page 229: bottom © Morten Bjarnhof; Page 244: top left © Robert Thomason, top right © Ole Haupt; Pages 246–247: top left, right and bottom left © Kim Hansen, bottom right © Anders Sune Berg